> This is an inspiring, educational and motivational book filled with true stories of security and adventure.

SECURITY.
ADVENTURE.
SERVICE.

INSPIRING YOU TO BE A CHAMPION GUARD

By Job Moses

Copyright © 2018 by Job Moses

All rights reserved. No parts of this book may be transmitted or reproduced, printed, shared, photocopied, and saved with any electronic or mechanical saving devices without the written consent of the Author.
For enquiries: jobmosesbks@gmail.com

Edited by Emma Moylan
Book Cover Design by TVN Designs
Formatting & Interior Design by Nonon Tech & Design

DISCLAIMER

The stories in this book are true stories. Stories I was part of, witnessed, confronted and even stopped; but they do not reflect the views of any particular organisation or entities.

I also wish to state, I do not support or condone any act of crime, violence or offence in any way or form. No matter how hilarious or funny they might have looked. My aim of writing these stories is to expose criminal acts, educate every individual who reads this book to better their security and be better security officer themselves.

ACKNOWLEDGEMENTS

Although my name is written on the cover as the author of this book, I must be quick to point out that without the support of so many people in my life over the years and in the course of writing it, I would not have been able to undertake such a project.

I will mention just a few, and to others I forget to mention, know that I will always acknowledge and regard you in my heart.

I would like to thank my beautiful wife, Deanne, who is an inspiration to me always. I love you, my love. I also thank my beautiful daughters, Shaniyah and Keila, for their support and patience during the many hours I spent writing. I love you both!

Not to forget my older brothers back in the mother continent, Bako, Emmanuel and Farouk, I miss you guys and I have the utmost respect for you all. I appreciate all the support and understanding you have shown me over the years. I love you guys!

I would like to thank Ian and Heather Nott for the many years of support, counselling, advice and being like my parents here in Australia. I also thank Ps Nicholas and Zara Jones, a great couple who have supported me and shown me love like I was their son. And to Michael Corrie, you are like an angel and a great friend.

I would like to thank my editor, Emma Moylan, for her patience and skill in turning what I have written (with English my third language) into something everyone can read and enjoy. I would also like to thank all the security companies, sites, supervisors, managers and team members who I have had the great privilege to work with and learn from over the years. Without your support, I wouldn't have been able to write about the everyday adventures the security officer experiences and goes through for the world to read and enjoy.

And to you reading this book, I would like to say thank you. I wrote it just for you!

TABLE OF CONTENTS

Disclaimer i
Acknowledgements ii
Foreword 1
Preface 2
    Story-Chased by Armed Robbers 4
Chapter One: Journey into Security 7
    Story-Train Trip and Fined Before Work 10
Chapter Two: Working on a New Site 12
    Story-Resign Intimidated, Return to Conquer 14
Chapter Three: Customer Service 17
    Story-Bully Patron and the Ex-WWE Star 21
    Story-Returned the Next Day Wearing Stolen Clothes 23
Chapter Four: First Aid 25
    Story-Wait for Police to Get Your Items Back 30
Chapter Five: Security Officer Communication 32
    Story-Taking Down my Car Rego 35
    Story-Ice Addict had to be Lobbed Outside 38
Chapter Six: Dealing with Nepotism 41
    Story-Assault Threatened, it Backfired 48
Chapter Seven: Restraining (Asphyxiation) 50
    Story-Drunken Manager Fighting Patrons 52
Chapter Eight: Standing Up for Others 54
    Story-Threatened, but I Wouldn't Back Down 63
    Story-Phoney Homeless and Liquor 66
    Story-Homeless and the Blanket 68
    Story-Confronted by Mr Muscle 70

Chapter Nine: Dispute Resolution 72
   Story-Who Owns the Fifty Bucks? 77

Chapter Ten: Respect for all Employees, Customers and Clients.. 78
   Story-Thief Almost Tasered Me 81

Chapter Eleven: Right Attitude Will Take You Places 83
   Story-Arrive Early or Meet Pharrell Williams 86

Chapter Twelve: Presentation, Exercise, Personal Hygiene 88
   Story-
   Story-Stole, Eating with Family After 91

Chapter Thirteen: Shift Work and Night Shifts 93

Chapter Fourteen: Dealing with Trauma, Injuries and Grief at Work 99
   Story-Stabbed with Screwdriver 103

Chapter Fifteen: Retail and Security 105
   Story-Thief and a Con Artist 113
   Story-The Day I Felt Like Quitting 117

Chapter Sixteen: Security Officer's Pay and Entitlements 120
   Story-The Undesirable Haircut 128

Chapter Seventeen: How to Lose Your Security Job 130
   Story-Security Officer Coming to Steal 136
   Story-Employee Losing Job for Stealing 138

Chapter Eighteen: Be Ahead, Study More 140
   Nugget & Story-Playing on the Psyche of the Offender 143
   Story-Theft, Locked Car, Sheriff 147

Chapter Nineteen: Life Outside Security 149

FOREWORD

The security industry is full of people working hard and long hours, so when I was asked to read this book by Moses Job (an ex-student), I was told it was full of his stories and I relished the opportunity.

The stories are his, told in a way we can all relate to.

It was wonderful to take a break, read and laugh, whilst memories of similar incidents in my career came back to me.

Richard Franks

PREFACE

I have had people say to me in the past, "Why don't you write a book?". Such statements often come when I share with them some of my adventurous or hilarious experiences in the security industry. Quite a few people have said that to me, but one particular day, I was at work and my workmate Ben said to me, "Why don't you write a book?". A few hours later, a customer who was walking by said to me, "I'm sure you must have seen a lot of things around here," and when I answered, "yes, I had seen quite a lot," she replied, "why don't you write a book?". I got home that same day and lying on the bed talking to my wife and sharing some stories and plans, she too said to me, "why don't you write a book?". Soon that day where I had three different people say the same thing to me, that I should write an account of my experiences, it triggered something inside me and I told my wife that I would write a book.

Over the years in the industry, I have had the privilege to advise, counsel and chat with a lot of people. Many were security guards who were kind of looking for the right direction to follow for their security career or even their lives. Others were customers and sometimes contractors. It is a rare privilege for someone to choose to give you their time to speak with them, advise them and sometimes open up to you about what they are thinking or that they need some sort of support from you.

I have always made sure I tried my best to speak words that will lift people up! Words that turn despair into hope, to try and let these people know that the future is much brighter than now and even their past.

As a result of this and my experience in the security industry, I feel I have learnt a fair bit that I would like to share. My experience, tips and words, I believe, will help make the security officer and everyone who reads this book want to dream and follow their dreams. While at the same time enjoying the hilarious and sometimes dangerous experiences of the security officer and the adventures that are encountered.

I also hope this book serves to educate those who are outside of the security industry or looking to join it. As well as those already in the security industry who are looking to improve their skills and knowledge. This includes those who are clients of security companies, so they might see things from the perspective of the security officer and better understand their efforts. In gaining a clearer understanding of the security industry and the officers on the ground doing the work, may everyone become better equipped to secure the rewards of a win-win relationship.

STORY
Chased by Armed Robbers

What a site... I'm enjoying my job because I am always given regular hours and management seem to be happy with my work.

But this eventful and memorable day at work will be one I won't forget in a hurry. The day was one where I was doing night shift at work and my workmate who I was on with that night was doing the site's mobile patrol. I decided to do my internal roving patrol. Although it's night shift, it's very important I carry out such patrols intermittently.

After completing my foot patrols, I went back into the office and I thought I'd do some CCTV monitoring to see what's going on around the site.

It was around 2 a.m. in the morning, and within a few minutes of me entering the office and checking the cameras, I saw two men wearing black balaclavas and carrying metal objects in their hands. They were entering the site through an entry that has a retailer who operates 24/7. In other areas of the site there are barricades that stop people gaining access after hours, but the 24/7 retailer section is an exception.

The whole situation looked unreal to me. It felt like this balaclava duo were a joke or were pulling some kind of stunt, but I also knew something serious was going to happen.

I decided to radio my workmate on his mobile patrol to inform him of what I was witnessing but I wasn't sure if I was clear enough for him to understand me on the radio, as I was still in shock and thinking what to do! I settled on a crazy idea. I thought these fellas are going to rob the 24/7 store, even though there is a guard inside the store that works for the retailer, so I had better go help him because I could get there before the police would be able to attend the scene.

I started running towards that store, then to my surprise, my balaclava friends were not interested in the cheap merchandise inside the 24/7 store, but rather they were entering the site and I assume heading towards the jewellery store that was closed. Now I was almost face to face with the two would-be robbers. The distance between us was about 20 metres. When I stopped, they both stopped too!

I thought after they had seen me they would turn back and run away. Perhaps I was thinking too much, or maybe I thought I was some kind of 'super officer to the rescue', but no, was I wrong! The two thieves decided to run after me with the crowbars they had in their hands. The moment I saw the crowbars, I decided it's best I run for my dear life. I ran into the corridor that leads to our office. They pursued me for a short distance but then when I turned back I couldn't see them running after me anymore.

Later, I decided to check the cameras and I discovered the would-be robbers decided to turn back the moment I went into the corridor that leads to our office. They kind of looked frightened the moment they lost sight of me and they ran back into a waiting getaway car and sped off.

All this happened within a minute or so. I would definitely not advise or recommend anyone try what I did. I would strongly recommend you remain in a safe place while you call and wait for the police to assist.

WHAT WE LEARNT

We discovered the barricade that could have stopped those robbers from gaining full access into the site had been left unlocked by the cleaners.

| SECURITY ADVENTURE SERVICE |

We also found out that a couple of weeks earlier, there had been a similar robbery in another site where the jewellery store was robbed. The section of the site where I stood face to face with the robbers was where the expensive jewellery stores were located, but the good news is, nothing was stolen and no one was injured or harmed.

Chapter One

JOURNEY INTO SECURITY

At a certain tough time in my life, I remember asking myself, what's going on? Why is it taking me so long to find a job? I'd been in Australia for just over a year and no one wanted to employ me. Then, I became frustrated and somewhat depressed!

I wanted to work, but it seemed no one wanted to hire me; then I heard of a family friend who just got their security licence — ding! A light lit up in my brain! All of a sudden, I knew that was the job I am supposed to do and I was confident of getting into it.

This is just a part of my story about how I came to be working in the security industry. Many of you are starting afresh after your business or place of employment closed down, many are just looking for a career switch, and many are simply seeking some form of adventure; but whatever it is you are looking for, security has got it all for you and I can tell you, don't be scared or ashamed. If security is what you think you want to go for, it is a career that is extremely rewarding and filled with adventure.

NOT JUST WHAT YOU SEE

There are security officers in almost every aspect of our modern world; from those working as concierge, armed escort and reception staff, to those working with presidents and prime ministers, private investigators, in aviation, and on cruise ships. The list goes on.

Security is exciting and so diverse! Being a security officer provides you with limitless opportunities and could take you places you never dreamed of or imagined you would get into.

EXCITING EXAMPLES!

Complete your course in Close Personnel Protection (bodyguard training) and a few months later you might find yourself being part of the bodyguard team for an A-list Hollywood star visiting your country. After working with them for a few days, the head of security for the visiting celebrity was impressed with your quality service and they offer you to come to work with them in California. A few months later you are in California working as a celebrity bodyguard.

Stories like this are very common in the industry. And not just working with celebrities, but with politicians, top executives, business moguls, and the like. Not only are you working as a security officer, but you are also now part of a broader network.

WHAT TO DO

It's not just about working with people of influence in society. It is also about passion for the job and the endless possibilities and opportunities the industry could present to you.

Don't put the carriage before the horse yet, be sure you want to work in the industry. Do some research regarding what area of security you would like to work in and ask a few experienced guards questions. And I mean a few and not just one, so you get a range of opinions, rather than only speaking to one experienced officer who, for example, doesn't like the industry or has had a bad experience and may end up dissuading you not to join.

Talk to a few people, ring a few security institutions, tell them about your background and what area of security you'd like to work in. Be open to receiving their suggestions and you could be greatly helped by accepting as many of their recommendations as possible.

If you are still not sure, but, are convinced you want to join security, then you can start as a basic security officer. Later, when you have a better understanding of the industry, then you can decide what area of security you might want to branch into.

STORY
Train Trip and Fined Before Work

One nice summer's day I was working with this mob who I wasn't sure whether was a legitimate security business or not. They never displayed any security business registration, and I was new to the industry, so my idea about the industry was very limited in terms of me knowing which company was legit or not.

They called me and asked if I was available to work at an office building where they were having issues with their lock-system. I obliged. The shift was to start after all employees had left work for the day.

I lived 30 kms outside of the city. I had no car and it would take me about one and a half hours to get to the job via a bus and train.

When I got the call, I was told to be there as soon as possible because the employees would be leaving work shortly. I was excited just to be getting a 12-13hour shift, depending on when the office managers turned up in the morning. I got suited up and took the bus to the train station. The train heading to the city had just arrived as I alighted from the bus, and so the boom gate between the bus and train station had also just come down. I had to wait for it to lift up before I could run into the train station, but the problem was the boom gate only goes up when the train leaves the platform. If that happens and I am not on this very train, I will have to wait another 30 minutes, and every minute counts. I need to be at this job site as soon as possible.

Being only a few years in Melbourne, I had no idea that it is a must to wait for the boom gate to automatically unlock before you can cross the track and enter the train station. There is an emergency entry point though that permits you to cross the track even if the boom gate is locked.

I had seen a few people use that emergency entry in the past, and I myself had used it before to catch a train that was about to depart, so I thought it was always okay to use such entry points.

Back to my story, I decided to be smart by using the emergency entry that leads to the train station across the train tracks. I ran quickly and boarded the train, sitting in the last carriage, feeling victorious and still breathing hard because of the run to catch it. Just within a few seconds of being on the train, a group of State Rail authorised revenue officers very politely welcomed me with a smile and said, "did you just use the emergency entrance at the boom gate to cross the train track and get into the train?". "Yes," I replied. They said, "well it's an offence in Victoria and we will be issuing you with a fine of about $300." I was devastated. The 12-13 hour shift I was to do would only fetch me about $210 and now before even starting the shift, I had already got a fine of over $300. I was very unhappy and tried to talk my way out of it using many stupid excuses to justify my actions, but the State Rail officers wouldn't take any of it.

I went to the shift sad in the knowledge I was working for Public Transport Victoria, for the fine they just issued me!

Chapter Two

WORKING ON A NEW SITE

As we are told 'change is the only constant thing in life', change should be expected. It is something we all go through in life. You would consider humans to be used to change since we all go through change at one stage of our life or another, but that's not the case. Change is often dreaded and often people act like it wasn't expected.

Starting with our first day at school and the memory of the mixture of excitement and fear of the unknown we felt! To now, when we are going to be starting at a new work site. And not just casual, ad-hoc work at a new site, but a permanent position.

We often ask ourselves, what should I expect from this new site, and from our supervisors, managers and co-workers?

Most times, such questions in our mind only increase and cause us to become tensed up. Especially if we are coming from another site that we've had a terrible experience at. But, for the guard starting new in security, they often don't have these questions or concerns! Compared to an experienced guard who's starting a new job or switching sites, the newbie in the industry is so keen to just have a job and get industry experience that his worries are more focused on learning from his experienced co-workers, so as to be able to do the job on their own.

I'd like to add that working at a new site can be exciting, tricky and filled with dread all at the same time! However, your focus should be more on yourself than what to expect. Why do I say 'yourself'? Most times when you go to any place new, the more level-headed and humble you are, no matter how much experience you do or don't possess, the more likely your new workmates will be willing to teach you new things, be friendlier to you and share with you all the tricks of your new site, so you can excel and feel at home there.

Try not to go and tell your new colleagues how the 'regional manager or some boss in the head office is your friend or relative'. The moment you do that, you are placing a barrier between you and your new workmates, and they may not be comfortable working with you or teaching you things that could make your task much easier.

Avoid going to your new-site and telling people how much experience you already have in the industry, especially if it's a long time. You may sound cocky, and don't forget no matter how much experience you have accumulated in the industry, you are a still a newbie at your new site. So stay low and keep your experience in your hat for the time being and people will be willing to teach and train you. The respect comes further down the track when they later discover you have actually had years of industry experience before joining them at the new site.

So, the bottom line is, humility will stand you in good stead at your new site. Be eager to learn and you will be taught fast. Ask questions, make sure you always have a pen and a notebook to write things down. Never be ashamed to ask questions.

STORY
Resign Intimidated, Return to Conquer

What an experience — one of the few I won't forget in a long time! This is because I have always taken delight in doing jobs and tasks that are tough and filled with adventure since in doing them, I gain a lot of experience and learn a great deal. Perhaps such jobs make you stronger as a person, wiser and build your character.

This situation was one that shaped me a fair bit. I was working in a shopping centre where you see unruly teenagers. They come just to make a name for themselves amongst their peers, doing crazy stuff, intimidating, robbing, bullying and assaulting security officers, which increases their street credibility with their gangs or peers.

I was doing my roving patrol when I met this young boy who was about 11 to 12 years old and sitting on a shop's massage chair. I had a good friendly chat with him and eventually, he stood up, asking me questions about his other friends and if I had seen them. Before I could reply to him, this stocky, tough-looking 17-year-old who had two other teenagers with him came right up to my face. I could see they were very high on some kind of prohibited drugs.

He came right up to my face and started making threats at me. There was not much I could say to him, and so I walked away. I informed my supervisor, who rang the police and then came with another guard to where I was.

This teenager, who would not stop his intimidation and threats, had assaulted a guard in the centre before.

The good thing is I had already found another job a few days earlier and was only doing two more shifts before I started my new job. I had only a few days left, but I couldn't endure another intimidation or threat, so sadly I could not finish the two remaining shifts. I decided I'd had enough. A bit shaken, I had to leave the site earlier than expected.

BACK TO WHERE I LEFT OFF

Fast forward to a few months later, that same workplace offered me a new position. But this time around, I had decided to be a good friend of the gym. Not because I wanted to fight. No. One of the easiest ways to lose your security licence is to be in a fight. My motive for going to the gym was to restore my self-confidence and sense of presence. When I had been threatened by the teenager a few months back, I had lost a lot of self-confidence, and so the gym did help me to regain some amount of self-assurance.

BEAUTIFUL DAY

It was New Year's Eve, to be precise, and while roving around, some patrons approached me and said, "the teenager over there with his group of friends seized my slab of beer". I went over there and it was my old nemesis, who was fuming and trying to intimidate me again. I looked at him straight in the eye and told him, "hey buddy, you can't intimidate me, and you have to give back the slab of beer back to its owners". I also asked another guard to call the police and report what was going on. My new level of confidence caused my old nemesis to become quite afraid. The police arrived, and I also issued the teenager with a 12-month banning-notice.

IT DOESN'T END THERE

Less than a month later while roving, I saw him again. He walked up to me and said, "I am very sorry for my actions towards you the other day". I said, "you have been banned from the centre but if you do anything stupid again you will be arrested". "I understand", he said.

A few weeks later, the Loss Prevention officers (LPO) of a retail store in the centre called me. It was regarding a male who was loading his bag with stock. I knew who it was because a few minutes earlier he had walked passed me while I was setting up some barricades. Based on the description they gave me, I told the LPOs his name and that I was on my way.

While he exited the retail store with the stock he just stole, a female LPO called him by his name and brought him back into the store. The police were called and my tough talking and threatening nemesis was literally crying and begging like a little baby. I sent a security officer with another banning-notice to increase his ban from 12 to 18 months because he was in violation of his previous ban, and this time the police charged him and took him to court.

Chapter Three

CUSTOMER SERVICE

Security has evolved over the years; gone are the days when a security personnel's star quality or attribute to getting a job is their size and muscle mass or how intimidating they look. With the advent of technology, the world has become more educated and people the world over have come to understand their basic human rights. If they feel they have been unfairly treated, they have the right to make a complaint or engage a lawyer and take the situation before a court of law.

No business wants to be sued or be given negative publicity due to the actions of one bully security personnel employee. For this reason, the security officer is expected in this day and age to be more of a customer service professional than anything else.

SERVICING CUSTOMERS

Customer service also implies that security personnel offer assistance to customers, listening to customers, answering customer questions, and directing customers to the right place to get further help.

It is very important for the security officer to understand that they represent the client/employer. They are one of the first points of contact between the customer and the client, so it is imperative that a good first impression is made. The way you respond to the customer could determine their business patronage in relation to the client. That, in turn, keeps the security officer employed, as well as possibly advancing their career progression as a result of consistent outstanding customer service delivery.

SUPERIOR CUSTOMER SERVICE

A lot of times, the security officer is caught up in a very tricky situation as someone who represents authority/management and also customer service personnel. The security officer must learn to juggle both responsibilities with great care and professionalism.

An example of this is when an unreasonable customer who looks to be affected by an intoxicating substance comes into the client's premises and engages with the security officer in an unruly manner. The officer must be calm at all times and understand customer service is expected as a response to the unruly customer's behaviour before any other appropriate legal step is taken to address the patron.

The officer must engage with the unruly customer with an open mind and empathy, as they could be going through a tough time. More often than not, such customers tend to calm down when the officer reacts to their unruly ways with a dignified response.

Take note that other customers may be watching the way you deal with this situation and others may be recording you on their mobile device. So, if it comes to a situation where the unruly customer must be evicted from the premises, it must be done in a humane and careful manner, and it must be done with the safety of other customers in mind. I would suggest if possible for the police to be called to evict the customer before trying to do it yourself and always call a backup officer or employee to assist you if it must be done by security directly.

Customer service is always required from the security officer no matter the situation. Customer service also implies having the customer's best interest at heart. That is why a superior customer service experience is always expected from all security personnel.

MEMORABLE EXPERIENCE

Your job as a security officer is to try your utmost to give every customer and client an unforgettable experience each time they engage with you: smiling, listening to customers attentively, repeating customers questions back to them to be sure you heard them right, and if possible, writing down their queries on a piece of paper. These are some of the elements you could apply as part of your customer service technique.

When you engage with the customer and client, it is important you present yourself as interested in their concerns or questions. It is important to show you are enjoying your job! Likewise, it is important when engaging the customer that you act in a professional manner at all times and give them the best customer experience at all times wherever possible.

LESS STRENGTH, MORE SERVICE

The 21st-century client/employer of the security officer has more of an interest in positive publicity and positive feedback. Positive feedback creates greater customer retention along with the acquisition of new customers, both of which, in turn, increases client/employer revenue. You, as a security officer, must invest more in improving yourself with the right attitude to offer a world class customer service experience to all customers and patrons. Your focus must be on your ability to deliver outstanding customer service and not on your muscle or strength.

Many security officers have lost their jobs due to reliance on their strength rather than on their brains to deliver quality customer service. The officer must understand there is no situation that cannot be resolved through careful engagement with the customer or patron.

No client wants to employ a security officer who will punch a customer, no matter the situation or provocation. However, they will be willing to employ an officer who does their best to engage with a customer in a courteous and professional manner at all times.

Take note: I am not trying to say physical strength is not sometimes required in the industry; if it's used legally and proportionately. I am merely pointing out, however, that clients are much more interested in an officer who is customer service inclined and focuses on customer satisfaction.

STORY
Bully Patron and the Ex-WWE Star

This particular story would have gone unnoticed by the security officers if not for the insurance company that compelled the actor to contact us for assistance before he could get his vehicle fixed by insurance.

It was one beautiful Saturday. The shopping centre was abuzz with shoppers and car-parking spaces were very limited because it's the weekend. On a day like today, a lot of people remain at home, while many others make it a day they all go out to do their shopping, especially families.

At that particular time, there was very limited parking due to some major works going on, so often you would find patrons seriously arguing because of parking spots. Trust me, I have seen some serious and crazy arguments between people over a spot to park their cars.

But this particular incident was indeed the most crazy, hilarious and shocking I have seen!

A customer had just finished their shopping and was about to drive out of the spot where they parked, when two other patrons in their cars came from both the left and right side of the outgoing driver, waiting to drive into the spot the moment the outgoing patron drove their car out. One of the patrons driving a sedan drove into the empty spot to park, but the other patron who had equally been waiting for the spot but missed out decided to jump out of their car. He was a big local bloke about 6'4" or thereabouts. He went and banged on the other patron's car with his fist, threw some punches at the car, the driver was a male of African appearance. He landed a couple of more punches and then stood back.

NOT THE END

The patron who was assaulted decided to take his time and park his car properly and then he jumped out of his vehicle. Well, the aggressive bully was waiting outside in anger and rage. But when the patron who was assaulted got out of his vehicle, he was standing around 6'4", a massive-tank who looked to be a bodybuilder. He went straight up to the other local bully who started the fight, picked him up from the ground, slammed him on the car, and gave him a few good punches. The bully ended up begging and apologising, but by the time the bully had got what he asked for, it had become obvious, the patron who was first attacked was an African-American ex-WWE wrestler in Australia on holiday! Although the kind of car he drove made him looked smaller while sitting inside it, when he got out of his car, you soon realised he's someone you don't toy with.

I have seen so many crazy fights, just because of car parking spaces, particularly during the weekend shopping frenzy, but this was indeed the craziest of them all!

STORY
Returned the Next Day Wearing Stolen Clothes

A wise doctor once told me, life is like a mountain and a valley; there are some seasons in your life when everything seems to be going well: marriage, new house, new car, promotion at work, having kids, an increase in finances, etc. That's when you are on the mountain.

But the valley is when you lose your job, there's a relationship breakdown, loss of a loved one, you're down with depression, you missed that promotion or contract, or you're ill with some kind of sickness, etc.

But the one thing is, both seasons have something unique in them for us to learn some of life's necessary lessons. The valley prepares you for life on the mountain because if you get to the mountain without passing through the valley, you might not be strong and resilient enough to maintain every good blessing life has to offer you on the mountain.

BACK TO THE STORY

Oh, let me not get distracted from my little story that sometimes makes my job as a security officer unique, because you see certain situations cause you to smile and wonder, 'what's going on?' Some days at work are hard and other days are just simply beautiful, just like my mountain and valley illustration!

| SECURITY ADVENTURE SERVICE |

It's a beautiful Melbourne day and I'm doing my job and enjoying the elegant centre I work in and the wonderful community that I have all around me. Next thing, I receive a call on my two-way radio to assist a retailer who's having some issues with a customer. I rushed there and I asked the retailer, "what's going on?" She tells me a female customer had just walked in wearing clothing they believe was stolen only the day before, and, it also looked like the female customer was here to steal again.

I approached the customer and had a cordial chat with her about the clothes she was wearing. She kind of claimed ignorance but the clothing still had the security tag on it; I wondered what kind of thief is this? You stole a few days before, forgot about removing the security tag and returned to the store wearing the same dress with the tag still attached.

I showed the lady the tag on the dress she was wearing. The retailer wants the dress back and the customer doesn't have a single cent on her. Are we in a quandary here or what?

This was a difficult situation to negotiate. I couldn't allow the clothes to be stripped off the offender because she would have to go home naked. But equally, I can't let her leave the store without either leaving behind the clothes or paying for them or at least leaving some kind of ID which she doesn't have with her. The retailer insists she wants her items back.

I felt the best thing to do was to be part of the story somehow, so I decided to ask for the price of the dress and I ended up paying for it. Both parties were happy and I escorted the offending lady out of the centre and warned her not to return again.

Chapter Four

FIRST AID

I remember when I was undergoing my first aid training to be a security officer. We were taught all kinds of good stuff to help us prepare and equip us to be excellent security personnel! First aid training, from my experience in the industry, is one of the most important trainings the security officer receives. One thing that is prevalent in this training delivery, however, is the rush many trainers and institutions are in to get through these courses without the proper equipment, training videos and other practical training materials necessary to make the student have that feeling of coming close to real-life first aid scenarios. Some of the schools that offer more in-depth training tend to be a bit pricey (which we can all understand why), but there are also a lot of training schools that seem to be in a rush just to get as many students in class as they can and make as much money as possible. They forget that the training they offer today could be a lifesaver in the future when their student is confronted with a real-life first aid emergency situation.

One of the proudest moments I have always had as a security officer is when I am carrying the Trauma Kit (first aid bag) and rushing to the scene of an incident that requires first aid. At that moment, everyone around tends to forget you are a security guard (or as we are sometimes called in ridicule, 'failed cop' or 'wannabe cop'). All that people see in that moment is not your security uniform or crowd control number, but that red bag you're carrying. You are one kind of 'saviour' at that moment of need because you are the first responder before even the ambulance or paramedics arrive.

IT WAS NEVER SO AT FIRST

Well, it was never so when I started as a security officer in the industry. Although I have always had a valid Basic or Level Two first aid qualification and have worked on many countless sites, my training was never called into action. Nevertheless, I always had this false confidence inside me that said, 'I'm first aid trained and I know how to do first aid'. That myth was broken not long after. My confidence was just a false illusion and my first aid certificate was not as valuable as a bubble gum sticker!

WHAT CHANGED IT ALL

After many years in security, here I was walking around with a secret arrogance and going to several jobs interviews bursting with confidence that 'I am an experienced guard', based on the books. I was an experienced officer, but in practical terms, regarding some of the most important things that matter, I was deceiving myself and others without even knowing.

Many security officers are like that today, and the question I ask is, 'do you know how to do first aid?' Having the certificate is different from knowing how to do practical first aid.

I'd just started a job at a new site. It was a shopping centre, that was my first time working in the retail industry. Mind you I have worked in some of the toughest security sites in the country (Exxon Mobil, GE Money, Formula 1 Grand Prix, Sea Port, etc.) and my first aid was never called into question.

This shopping centre was just a few minutes' walk from my home, so I was really pleased to have such a job close to home. What changed it all, was one day there was a first aid emergency call (known as Code Blue on site). The duty supervisor asked me to attend to the incident (take note, in that site I was new, but I had been in the security industry longer than about 60% of the officers on that particular site) so I took the Trauma Bag, went there, met the injured patron lying on the floor, then I opened the bag...........boom! I almost required first aid myself because of how confusing the number of items was that I saw inside the bag. I had only a few seconds to ask the injured patron questions and to decide what to apply on her or what to do. Meanwhile, there are other customers who were watching, anticipating for me to do something and here I was 'super guard', confused, and not having a clue what to bring out of the bag to apply on the customer. I'm sure the lady thought I was a joke of a guard and she decided, 'I think I am better now,' without my first aid. Seems she got better just by watching my comic display and panic of not knowing what to do, or at least that's what I thought.

I was relieved when the customer left. I was sweating and I left there too myself, embarrassed, but at the same time, I found it funny!

So many officers that later came to that site found themselves in a similarly embarrassing situation to the one I had found myself in. Sadly, it's not a situation that's funny, because that experience I had was something minor. The lady had a little cut so it wasn't something serious that could have gotten me into trouble.

WHAT'S THE SOLUTION?

History has shown that people tend to learn from mistakes, past experience and from hindsight. I learnt a very valuable lesson from that experience:

<u>Ask questions</u>: Training at school gives you mainly a paper certificate and not life experience. So, when you go to work, look for some of the most experienced guards on site, be it the team leaders, supervisors or managers. Be humble and tell them you would like them to give you some first aid tips based on their years of experience, through some of the basic and challenging first aid situations that they've encountered. How did they approach such incidents? What was the outcome and what did they learn from such experiences?

Familiarise yourself: Talk to experienced work personnel on site. Tell them you would like them to help you familiarise yourself with the trauma bag/first aid kit. There are so many medical items inside the bag, some you haven't seen before. Ask about each and every item—what is their name, and what do you use them for? If possible, practise this again once a week until you become familiar with each and every item.

I would recommend that supervisors and managers complete this procedure, or as designed by the site, with each and every new/old employee. The procedure should consist of going through the trauma bag with your security personnel and making sure they know the medical items that are inside the bag and what their uses are. It could be monthly, quarterly or annually depending on what your management and site agree on.

Watch others: Always follow experienced guards and staff to first aid emergencies and watch how they apply first aid. Watching them gives you great insight and knowledge. What they are going through, and if you can follow them as often as possible that would help to build your confidence and experience in handling future emergency first aid situations you might be attending alone.

Self-development: Try to personally obtain pictorial first aid books as approved by your state, territory or country and go through them in your spare time at home. There are YouTube videos and DVDs produced by training organisations with medical body certification that you could spend a few hours a week watching in order to gain more knowledge and to improve your skills in first aid.

I AM JUST A SECURITY GUARD, WHY FIRST AID?

When people make a mockery of you as a security officer it's because they don't understand or know the value you add to a business or community. You are first aid trained and sometimes your response and approach to a medical emergency is what decides whether the injured or unwell person will live or die. I make this statement from personal experience. I have been involved in situations that were life and death, and where first aid skill is what kept the patrons alive before paramedics arrived and took over the situation.

So that's why it's important for security personnel to have lots of first aid experience. Moreover, your first aid skill could also be required at home, on the highway, in parks and in so many situations and places when you're not even at work and that could also save someone's life.

STORY
Wait for Police to Get Your Items Back

Once again, I'm walking down to the shopping centre and enjoying the privilege of working in this beautiful site! Seeing lots of different faces, some are new, others are regulars. Observing kids playing around, others throwing tantrums on the floor and who won't move from that spot. You can see from the faces of their parent's that they are exhausted and they just want to complete their shopping in peace and go home. All the parents want is to find the best bargain and save as much money as possible for the family.

BACK TO THE STORY

I see a lot of things daily and I am often enriched by these experiences. Then comes the moment my teammate and I were roving around and we found someone had left a 20-inch TV under a table that's meant for diners. We picked it up and took it to the service desk in case its owners came for it.

Our control room operator reviewed the CCTV footage and the people that left the box were identified. They had been in the centre earlier acting really weird while the box was in their possession.

A few minutes later a male came for the TV and we asked him to present some ID so we can record his details before giving him back the TV. He refused to and said, "I have no ID on me," then I said, "don't worry we have got few police officers on site, they will be here shortly and you can have your item back". The male said, "okay, look, I have to go and catch my bus, "before I could tell him to wait, he ran off.

An hour or so later he returned with his female partner who said she had an ID—a passport, and I said, "have you got any ID with an address on it?" He said she didn't have and we kept on arguing. We then asked both of them to give us their mobile contact number so we could save it just in case something comes up about the TV later but she said, "no I don't have credit on my phone and I don't know the number off the top of my head." I said, "okay wait for the police and it won't be long before you will have your items back." The moment we mentioned the police again they just bolted away and left the TV behind.

WEIRD SITUATION

Most times we give owners their lost and found items back without any fuss. During this particular period though, we had lots of police patrolling in the centre, assisting security as they do every so often. We could sense there was something weird about this couple, so we either wanted proper identification or to get the police to give them their items back, but it seems they were allergic to the word 'Police'.

Chapter Five

SECURITY OFFICER COMMUNICATION

A security officer is in the business of communication as the established job description of the officer states, 'Observe and Report'. So a big part of your job is to witness and to communicate.

A good number of individuals come into the industry without realising that you need to learn how to communicate in the security guard way, and often in a site-specific way. Regardless of what your background is before joining the security industry, you must be willing to learn the industry and site-specific ways and modes of communication.

Below are some of the tools and modes through which security officers communicate within the industry.

Two-way radio: Radio is one of the most important ways for the security officer to communicate onsite and for that reason, I often call them the security officer's best weapon. Not lethal but effective in keeping officers informed and the site safe.

As a new guard if you haven't used a two-way radio in the past, before commencing your shift, ask an experienced officer, supervisor or manager to show you how to use the radio. Sometimes an older guard might have difficulty in using a new radio in a different site due to a change of brand, technology, frequency or other factors.

Always feel free to ask questions, as some sites use the radio differently, such as the use of security-phonetic alphabets, for example, that others don't employ. Ask for your call sign and if possible the call signs of people you will be directly reporting to.

Communication books: A number of sites have communication books; it could be a physical book, or other times an online version.

This book primarily covers communications between officers; from guards completing their shift to a new officer starting their shift. Other sites may have additional uses for such books than the one mentioned here.

Security notebook: This is another vital book to always carry around; some security firms have company-specific notebooks they issue their guards, while others allow the officer to purchase one themselves.

It's very important to carry this notebook with you at all times when you are working, ensuring it is stored in a safe place after work or when it's filled up.

The notebook is important for writing down briefs of incidents and for taking the details of people involved in the incident at that particular moment before you complete an incident report.

Phones: Mobile phones have become one very important tool for the security officer; not just to make phone calls, but also for taking pictures and capturing video of incidents, hazards or anything that could be a safety or health concern for patrons, clients or employees.

I could write a whole lot on why it's important to always carry your phone with you as an officer, but I am sure most of us already know the importance of always having your mobile devices with you. It could save a life or capture very good evidence to settle any future disputes.

Mobile phones also come in handy in case of faulty or insufficient two-way radio coverage onsite or where there is the need for a more private conversation between the officer and control, other officers or management without everyone listening in on such a conversation.

Email: I always encourage people when communicating with their employers or superiors (especially on important subjects) at work to put it in writing because there have been cases where the other party says, 'you never informed me,' or, 'I am not aware'. Email is an effective way to communicate; records are kept on both the sender and receiver's devices and can be accessed easily where there is a computer, mobile phone or tablet with an internet connection.

Email has many significant uses for the security officer, but I'm focusing here on the importance of record keeping when communicating via email.

<u>Sign-in/crowd control book</u>: It's essential for every guard when on duty to sign in at the commencement of their shift and sign off at the end of their shift. That's one of the main purposes of the sign-in book. The sign-in book could also be used for legal purposes to confirm that the security officer was at work at the day and time registered in the book, so always sign it.

<u>Timesheets</u>: I'm sure you want to get paid after you have completed your shift? A security officer's record of hours worked needs to be signed and then passed on to the payroll department to pay the officer's wages.

I have witnessed officers not being paid or being underpaid because of various discrepancies owing to the site or security company having no timesheets. But if you complete the hours worked in the timesheets, you have the surety of being able to refer to it if you're having issues with your pay. In other instances, the employer may refer to it to help them recoup overpayments to the officer.

STORY
Taking Down my Car Rego

You know any job you enjoy doing, you will always do it right. And often I tell people, no matter the job you find yourself doing at a particular moment of your life, always do it with grace and delight and people will definitely see distinction and excellence in what you do!

Great workplace dramas are often not far from the security officer. If it is stories to tell, a security officer can tell you an abundance of them that will make your day, and change the way you view certain things in life.

TO MY STORY

This couple came to the point I would refer to as 'red line patrons'. That's a patron that you are always 99% sure when they visit your site that they will cause trouble or commit an offence.

This particular couple were both in their late teens or early twenties. They were tall, but they looked very much like people experimenting with drugs. They often came to the shopping centre to shop, but at the same time were always looking for the slightest opportunity to steal.

I know them and most officers around know them too. I took a special interest in this couple because I have received lots of calls from so many retailers regarding them stealing or trying to steal. Each time I see them I always make my presence known. By roving around so they become uncomfortable and they are aware I am watching them. They sometimes then leave, but at other times confront me, yelling and calling me names.

I did that as often as I saw them in the centre, and not only them but any 'red line patron'. It's just part of our response to prevent theft, and sometimes we escort these 'red line patrons' out of the centre before they even steal.

OUTSIDE WORK

One day I had to go to update some of my medical records at Medicare (Australian healthcare) but Medicare share the same office as Centrelink (Australian social services), so I met my 'red line couple' friends in the Centrelink queue. Although they were there before me, they somehow knew where I parked my car and while they were leaving they took down the details of my car registration.

AT WORK

A few days later, I saw them at work and they reminded me that they'd taken down my car registration, maybe trying to intimidate me. But no, I wasn't going to get intimidated; I straight away kicked them out of the centre once again because I know what they are trying to get into.

LESSON LEARNED

Not all security work is dangerous, but there are times in some of the jobs I did, where I could not visit a lot of recreational parks and public places with my kids, because of the fact that I did my job well and with confidence. Sometimes I would see some of those colourful characters that I have encountered at work at these places, so I would just drive somewhere else.

Though I am very careful, I take delight in doing my job and don't really have much time to focus on threats. As long as I deliver to my employer and client, that's what gives me deep satisfaction!

STORY
Ice Addict had to be Lobbed Outside

I remember my workmate once said to me, "have you realised almost anytime you are at work, we always have to deal with some unique situation?" That's pretty true, I said. Well, that's part of the reason I felt motivated to write a book.

BACK TO THE STORY

This particular story was kind of funny, tough and placed us security personnel on the edge during and after the whole incident!

I was doing my regular foot patrols with one of my security colleagues, who I will call Dwayne. We were patrolling the car park when we saw this old model red Ford Falcon pull into the parking lot with two roughly-dressed males sitting in the driver and passenger seats.

The male sitting in the passenger side drank a large can of an energy drink and then threw the can out on the floor. Dwayne said to me to ask him to pick it up. Well in the line of security duties, the body language of customer/patrons largely determines how you communicate with them. At this point, I could read their body language to be one looking for trouble, so I moved the can to a place where it wouldn't litter the area as much or be a hazard to others, then we walked away.

A few minutes later I got called by a retailer; there are some customers who looked drunk and are being disruptive. I rushed into the store and saw the first 'customer'. He looked okay, but the other male looked disruptive and I was told he'd stolen something and hid it in his pocket. I asked for the items back but this 'customer' denied stealing and continued being disruptive.

I perceived that this customer was affected by illicit drugs and he could cause many problems if allowed to remain in the store, so I decided to focus on trying to get him to leave. He did leave with his friend without returning the stolen item and the shop owner was not happy with my decision, but I told her it's better we get him to leave than to keep arguing with someone whose state of mind is beyond being rational and may end up causing more damage and loss for her business. She reluctantly accepted my judgement.

About 20 minutes later, I received a call about a customer who had stolen some items from another store and walked out. A few minutes after that I got yet another call about a customer stealing items from a different store. All descriptions pointed to it being the same drug-affected person I had dealt with earlier.

I sent other security officers to search for this male with his accomplice. His accomplice had left the centre alone in the car, leaving his drug-affected friend behind, although his current whereabouts were unknown.

15 minutes later we received another call, of a male peeing right at the front of the centre entry. Customers had complained so we had to rush into action.

I rushed there with my supervisor and Dwayne, then our security manager joined us too. I met this male inside a $2 store. He had all the stolen items in his hands, and the new store items in his hands too, which he claimed he had paid for. But he was lying and he hadn't paid for them. I asked him to leave the store because of his previous multiple thefts.

He became very belligerent, and the next thing we know he punched Dwayne who was on the phone with the police. Well, where I work, when you physically attack a security officer, customer or client, then you have crossed the line and we will ask you to leave or physically remove you from the centre for the safety of everyone.

So the 'meth-man' gave us no choice but to physically remove him from the store and centre. One security officer alone would not have been able to do it, so three of us had to remove him and had him restrained outside the centre until about eight police officers arrived and arrested the male for theft, assault and urinating in public.

Though I tried as much as possible to write most of these true stories accurately; bringing the tension, fear, struggle and danger we face to life, it's really hard to use words to do so, because being in that situation and experiencing these tough episodes within a short few seconds or minutes is sometimes surreal!

People who are on methamphetamine are some of the most difficult patrons you will have to deal with, and you have to be prepared to protect everyone else, including the drug affected person. If possible, take the person to an isolated place that won't draw unnecessary attention and make sure you restrain such patrons professionally so you don't cause asphyxiation.

Chapter Six

DEALING WITH NEPOTISM

Drake is the manager of the security site. He loves his job. He's got about eight full-time permanent guards working under him and two assistant managers for support. Later, one of the assistant manager positions becomes vacant. Two senior and experienced officers were in line to be made an assistant manager (Tom and Chris). However, Drake decided to make Carver, who he's been friends with from a different site, the assistant manager to fill the vacant position.

Carver is not among the two senior experienced guards. Carver has no vehicle, so he's always arriving to work late. The guards are not able to complain because Carver and Drake are very close friends. Drake won't even entertain any complaint about the appointment or Carver's lateness to work daily. Did I forget to mention that Carver has also got minimal experience on that site? Welcome to nepotism. Voilà!

Are you familiar with the above story or something similar in a place where you work or have worked before? Nepotism/cronyism is one of the biggest issues within the security industry, after underpayment of wages.

Nepotism means that due to friendship or closeness of a superior with a subordinate, that the superior favours, gives opportunity, promotion or employment to the subordinate even when they are not the most qualified, and sometimes not capable of doing the job.

Sometimes nepotism has this face: the boss will decide from among three senior employees due for training. The boss will pick their friend who is among the three, choosing to train them and disregard the other two, depriving them of the necessary training or coaching they are due. In that way, their friend might then stand out among the three.

Nepotism has so many different forms and faces. Depending on who the boss is, they to do it either openly or subtly.

DARK SIDE OF NEPOTISM

Quitting employment: Nepotism has made so many security officers quit their jobs. It has made many officers depressed because their skills, contribution and talent is never recognised or acknowledged because they're not friends with the boss, yet they do their job professionally and go home without sucking-up to anyone.

Discouragement: Nepotism at workplaces causes a lot of discouragement among hard-working employees because due process is not being followed. As a result, the hope of the hard-working officer is being diminished and they see no reward for their efforts and dedication.

Conflict at work: One of the easiest ways for there to be employee disharmony at work is once there is an opportunity for promotion and career progression and the only relevant qualification of the person who succeeds in being promoted is 'boss's friend', then conflict starts at work, employees stop respecting their boss or at least they are forced to do so.

Discipline: I have seen situations at work where the friend of the boss consistently keeps violating workplace codes of conduct or standard operating procedures and the boss never takes any action with their friend, even when other employees report the violations and flawed behaviour. Sometimes a whitewash meeting could be held and everyone knows nothing will be done about it. Instead, the employee who made the report may end up being victimised.

So, disciplinary actions only apply to other employees and not the friend/relative of the boss.

REDUCED PRODUCTIVITY

Promotes laziness: Often beneficiaries of nepotism/cronyism tend to be one of the laziest employees. They are only hardworking when the boss or management are around, known as 'eye service'. After they are gone they won't raise a finger to work but will be barking out commands to other employees.

The other face of laziness is when the idle officer knows the boss likes employees that suck up to them, then you see them not being active with their duties but investing enormous amounts of time and energy sucking up to their bosses. Other employees then suffer because they end up doing most of the lazy officer's tasks while they're dedicating their time to sucking up to the boss.

Lack of respect: You see when that employee who benefits from nepotism/cronyism is being promoted; people tend to have little respect for them or for the boss who enabled such a negative workplace culture to go on.

People are simple. When an employee's talents, skills and hard work earns a position, people tend to recognise such a person and more respect is accorded to the boss who made the right decision to promote the deserving employee!

Lack of trust: How can you trust a boss who subscribes to nepotism/cronyism? When you know the boss or an employee won't do what is right, how can they be trusted when it comes to something serious or important?

NEPOTISM/CRONYISM GOES AROUND

I have observed with time and experience that a lot of bosses who practice or enable nepotism tend to be people who were once beneficiaries of nepotism themselves. So, when they get to the position of power they tend to look for or entertain any minions who are willing to suck up to them and then later reward them.

NEPOTISM DESTROYS TALENT

<u>Looking elsewhere</u>: Many businesses have lost so many great talents in their fold because of nepotism. Skilled and talented employees often start looking elsewhere the moment they perceive their talents are underutilised or rubbished.

<u>Hidden talents</u>: A lot of great talents in the industry have been so discouraged because of the prevalence of nepotism/cronyism at workplaces. Their heart is not fully dedicated to their jobs or they try to hide their talents and ideas that could move their place of employment to the next level of growth.

<u>Wrong positions</u>: So many skilled and talented employees are placed in the wrong department/position because where they are supposed to be working and utilising their skills is being occupied by a beneficiary of nepotism/cronyism. How do you expect a square peg to fill in a round hole?

YOUR FRIEND/RELATIVE CAN BE PROMOTED

I am not talking about bosses at workplaces who promote employees who are qualified, experienced and talented to positions that have become vacant even though the employee promoted is their own friend/relative.

I am talking about employees that a kangaroo in the outback of Australia will read their resume and reject them from babysitting a joey. An employee that does not deserve or is not qualified for the position and promotion but they end up getting promoted because they know someone.

TACKLING NEPOTISM/CRONYISM

Be warned: It can be dangerous tackling nepotism/cronyism. It often fights back and it could lead to the loss of your job, depression, discouragement, or loss of favour and promotion with bosses.

First, count the cost before venturing into this battle. If you're not sure you can win, I will advise you not to go into this fight.

If you decide to fight it, do so respectfully, even though those on the other side tend to follow no rules when fighting back.

Bosses: You can have friends/relatives at work and still do what is right. It's said 'charity begins at home', but when people report your friend to you for doing the wrong thing, be open-minded about it and do what is right so you will set a good example for others. For if you do not spare your friend and instead discipline them, then everyone will be in line and do the right thing.

When your friends are not deserving of promotion or position, don't promote them or even recommend them.

Friend/relatives of the boss: 'Do unto others as you would have them do unto you.' (Matthew 7:12). That Bible verse resonates with every human today, whether you are faith inclined or an atheist. One thing I am sure of is you would want others to treat you with respect and dignity. Basic human rights.

You have to understand your actions of wanting to take a shortcut to the top are not right and it's hurting a lot more people than you know.

You have to understand you are painting your boss/friend in a bad light because of your selfish ambition.

You have to understand you can get to the top through hard work and dedication without sucking up to anyone and people will respect you more at the top when it's your hard work that gets you there.

How would you feel if a younger relative later in life comes to you and tells you how their talents at work are not being appreciated and rewarded and they feel like quitting their job or they end up being depressed? You have to do things today and also think of tomorrow, because if a bad culture of nepotism doesn't get stopped by you, kids of today may suffer from such negative workplace culture tomorrow.

Employees: A lot of great patience is required here, you must be careful how you deal with cronyism/nepotism and study your workplace before taking it head-on.

Speak to the beneficiary: If you think it's possible and they will listen, speak to your boss's friend about how their actions are not right and are affecting other employees. Do not abuse them but speak to them with empathy and respect. Sometimes they've got no idea their actions are wrong until someone tells them.

Speak to your boss: I know you might be deeply hurt and sometimes think they won't listen to you, but I will encourage you to speak to them about how their actions or their friend's actions are causing issues for other employees.

Speak to them respectfully whether they will accept your concern or not. The reason you speak to them is for them to be aware of their friend's actions, of employee dissatisfaction and also just in case you end up taking the matter to senior management so they know you followed due process of reporting.

Senior management: You must try to ascertain if the person your boss reports to is someone who will entertain and listen to your valid complaints because sometimes the boss and his superiors are in cahoots and share a similar negative culture.

Band yourself together: I would encourage all affected employees to band themselves together, 'a cord of three strands is much stronger than two'. Often the more numbers you have to report your dissatisfactions with nepotism/cronyism at work, the more likely your boss and workplace will take you seriously and address it.

<u>Look for another job</u>: It's sad I have to recommend this option! I believe that every employee is in their position to ameliorate their workplace no matter how long you manage to stay at your place of employment.

YOU TRIED

I believe everyone is a change agent for good and doing the right thing in life gives more satisfaction than money.

You have made an effort to see change and the right thing being done at your workplace and nothing seems to change and the good guy is now seen as the bad guy.

Well, here is good news, you haven't failed! You challenged a negative culture and you gave it your best shot. Even though other employees may not say it to your face, they do admire your boldness, fearlessness and courage.

Now try looking for another job that you think you would love to do. Maybe a change of career or start your own business. As I always say, be sure it's what your heart wants and you think you will enjoy doing it. An occupation where your skills and talent will be greatly appreciated and rewarded. Go for it, and don't regret your actions for wanting to see wrong-gone and right-done!

STORY
Assault Threatened, it Backfired

I believe when your heart makes the effort to always wanting to do what is right, then there is nothing to be afraid of and no threat should make you lose sleep, because your aim is to have clean hands.

This girl, I will call her Siam, she worked in one of the fast food restaurants in the centre. On so many occasions, while she was on her days off from work, she engaged in the habit of shoplifting from other retail stores in the centre. Surprised? Don't be. I have seen a few cases like that; work in the centre in the morning, by noon stealing from there!

Siam's case was really bad, because she not only shoplifts, she assaults people, threatens the security officers and always throws in, 'I work here in the centre'. What an irony right? Working in the centre should make you more responsible, careful and conduct yourself in a manner that would not affect your employment, but for her, it's a kind of a licence to steal.

Siam has got a plethora of theft reports against her name. To some extent, I would say some officers in the centre were afraid to deal with any incident that she was involved in due to past history of threats and assault. She normally came with a large group of girls and she was like their ringleader. They walked into multiple stores stealing; threatening and sometimes assaulting staff members.

I got called about a large group of girls who had just stolen from a retailer. I tracked the girls on CCTV and saw it's Siam and her group. I followed her into another retail store and I knew they were up to no good there. So I had a chat with her and she wouldn't return the stolen items from the last store they just left, but rather she was telling me, "if you get me angry I will slap you." Yes, I have received a lot of such threats before and I have seen security officers being slapped, bloodied and on other occasions, ambulances have been called to treat guards because someone assaulted them.

I wasn't scared by such a threat. If I get scared of them then who gets to protect the helpless retailer before the police arrive? Besides, I had a few guards for backup; I always try to have backup. I insisted she and her group leave the centre and we escorted them out.

About an hour later, a major supermarket called security to report that they have got a large group of girls stealing in their store. I checked the cameras and I discovered again it was Siam and her group. This time they were very disruptive and Siam even had a screwdriver with her.

I went into the store with a couple of security workmates. I evicted the group and Siam assaulted one of the retail managers. She showed off the screwdriver and kind of letting the guards know that she's got a weapon. I managed to disarm her and kicked them all out of the centre and called the police. Yes, they did steal a few items, and we recovered a few back.

Police swiftly came, took their details and went on to investigate them and the whole incident.

I wrote a comprehensive report about Siam's activities. Did I mention other officers had tried getting Siam banned from the centre but failed because her fast food chain employer kept protecting her? This time around my security manager used the report I sent, pressed the police and Siam's employer to act on it. She lost her job and the police issued a warrant for her arrest because she was also involved in other theft elsewhere.

Chapter Seven

RESTRAINING (ASPHYXIATION)

The security industry has copped a lot of abuse by members of the public who think the average security officer as a licensed thug or bully walking around and looking to take undue advantage of patrons.

The industry has also been hurt from within: by officers, who are heavy-handed, officers who are ill-trained, and also by officers who go outside of their approved training, legislation and site procedures to do things in ways that end up affecting their jobs, employers and the security industry as a whole.

The majority of officers in the industry are some of the best we have around, but there is always that little minority who gives the industry negative press by their actions.

RESTRAINING

The industry has suffered from negative publicity by officers who have restrained patrons illegally or in the wrong way. That is why every officer in the industry must be careful when it comes to restraining patrons and if possible they should be properly trained on restraint techniques.

Asphyxiation simply means denying someone airway breath. When restraining goes wrong that's when you find the security industry on the bad side of the news, companies losing contracts and guards' taken to court and even sometimes losing their licence or getting jail time.

BE CAREFUL

If you haven't got sufficient experience in restraining someone and you are not comfortable restraining an offending patron, I would advise you not to do it. I would suggest you immediately report to your immediate superior and call for backup. Never try to be a hero in a situation you are not trained to deal with.

You may need to watch a few YouTube videos of security restraints that have gone badly and see cases where the patrons lost their lives because of some overzealous security officer.

At any time you are engaged in restraining a patron and they tell you they can't breathe, stop immediately! It's better for the offender to get away than for you to be charged and go to court.

GET TRAINED

If you are ever in doubt of your restraining skills, I suggest you undertake a Restraint Tactics course or self-educate yourself with government recognised training institute's videos or manuals, or talk to an experienced officer in the industry and have them coach you on how to legally restrain an offending patron.

Take note: it is better not to restrain anyone than to restrain in the wrong way, because the moment you are thrown before the magistrate, most likely the client and your employer will forget you ever existed and get someone to take over your role, so be careful and be sure you know what you are doing.

STORY
Drunken Manager Fighting Patrons

I saw a security job advertisement on Gumtree and I decided to go for it, as I wasn't ready to find regular and permanent work just yet.

Most big companies when you newly start in the industry, they will tell you 'we want experience'. The few places willing to give you a go, sometimes are those companies you're not sure if they are legitimate or not.

The person with the job available told us it's a nightclub, about 70 km from my home. Well, I had no car, so the train was my best mode of transporting myself. I took the train and went to Cranbourne from where I live.

I met with the 'owner of the security company', that's if it was a real company! He told me and a few other guards, "I'm sorry, the place you will be working is not here but in Moe." That's about 170 km from where I live.

Despite my discovery of the new distance to the gig, I still could not turn down the job. I had spent the little money I had with me for the train ticket, and I would be at a loss, after all, it's the weekend and I have got nothing to do that night at home.

The problem is, I don't have a car to take me to Moe, but a guard who usually works in that nightclub volunteered to give me a lift. I was very elated to hear that! Halfway through our journey to Moe, my 'generous new friend' told me I have to pay him petrol fees for taking me there and back. I was shocked because he never mentioned that while we were at Cranbourne, though I was grateful for his assistance and I could understand why he wants me to pay half the cost!

Moe is a quite beautiful town that's about 136 km from Melbourne. We arrived there at about 10 p.m., so most stores in town had already closed.

We went straight to the pub that also has the nightclub. The whole place looked kind of strange to me, as most people at the club were country folks. I just started having the feeling of wanting everything to end as quickly as it could, so I can go home.

The night went well and I was pleased by how everything went. Then we were about to sign off when suddenly I heard people screaming outside. I knew it was a fight so I decided to go check what's going on. I realised the manager of the venue, who was seriously intoxicated was busy punching someone, a patron on the floor and another crazy security officer (the guard who gave me the lift) was there assisting the manager to pin the patron down.

The manager sort of sat on the patron and he was kind of struggling to breathe. The manager expected me and another security officer that came, to assist him in assaulting the patron. We both declined, and rather, I took the manager off the patron before he became asphyxiated.

The manager wasn't too happy with me and the other guard! But for me, as long as I stopped something illegal continuing, then I was happy with the decision I took.

A week later, I realised I hadn't been paid for that job and the owner of the 'security company' told me what the manager had said. He won't pay because we refused to help him. He means help him beat up a patron.

I eventually got paid, but only after I explained to the 'security company' owner what actually happened.

Chapter Eight

STANDING UP FOR OTHERS

Security is a very interesting and drama-filled industry, which has many great individuals and others with colourful and shifty personalities. You may find yourself in a workplace with a negative work culture that most likely has been brought in by the supervisor or manager, or the leaders there are enablers of such negative behaviour. Other times this negative culture and attitude are cyclical, brought in by a previous individual/leader and the circle continues going around and around.

Different sites have different challenges or negative cultures that prevail there. Sometimes such cultures are not just isolated to a particular site in the business, and the whole company could be caught up in this negative cycle.

Such negative behaviours include but are not limited to:
- Bullying
- Discrimination
- Victimization
- Sexism
- Racism
- Cronyism/nepotism
- Drug use
- Intimidation and harassment
- Wage theft

Take for example, several years ago, while I was just new in the industry, there was this security officer working with us at an event, but the trousers they were wearing had a different security company name written on them. I was told about that company, how a lot of negative stuff goes on there. Over the years that followed, I have met several guards who have worked or are working for this same security company, and all of them have similar negative stories/experiences regarding that particular XYZ company.

I later conducted a little enquiry. It seems the said business has a ton of negative press about them, and you can see that this negative culture could have started from the top and flowed down to bottom.

HOW DO I CHANGE IT?

Often people tend to believe 'nothing can be done about the negative situation because it's been so for ages,' but that's not true.

Something can be done about it and you are that someone that will have to help change things. Many years ago, women were never allowed to vote in Western democracies, but people campaigned and challenged the status quo. Today women can vote and contest for elected positions, and also be presidents and prime ministers of their respective nations.

I can go on, giving examples of historical situations that looked impossible to change, but everyday people, who mustered a bit of courage, stood up and called for change! E.g. Martin Luther King (U.S. civil rights movement) and William Wilberforce (abolition of slave trade in Britain).

I know you may be wondering why am I referencing great historical situations and figures, and you may say it's just 'security'. Well, you have to understand those historical figures were just normal people like you or me, but they were people who believed that injustice and negativity cannot continue to prevail, and so they stood up, not for just themselves, but for others and for those not yet born.

You, as a security officer are privileged to be doing what you are doing today. Not everybody in our society can be entrusted with the task of even securing a 'cup of coffee', either due to personal reasons or a criminal record against their names. It takes courage and inner strength to be a security officer. You find security officers being entrusted by the client to look after multi-billion dollar properties or investments, and so that's why I say it's a privilege to be a security officer.

So, if so much can be entrusted into the hands of a security officer to look after, why can't the security guard want for a better workplace, a positive work culture, respect for all employees, right pay and the opportunity for career progression?

With all the above questions asked, and if the security officer can make their place of employment a better place to work daily, then the client will get the best out of the security officers, and the security company will get a positive vibe, good feedback and attract the best officers to work for them and stay longer.

But how do you instigate that change? The purpose of everything I outlined above is for officers to realise their value, the privileged position they occupy, and why it is worth fighting to see a positive change happen at their workplace.

You need the following to succeed in your quest for change:

<u>Integrity</u>: This means being honest and having a great moral principle. Integrity is a very important attribute to have as a person and at work. People will trust you and believe the words you speak and the vision you project. Although these days it's a very uncommon attribute to find, my advice is to engage less in careless speech and behaviours at a workplace where everyone is trying to get ahead of others by hook or crook.

I remember a new site I was working at, and one of the employees told me, "when you do something wrong, never take responsibility for it, pass it to someone else." He was kind of telling me that in joking way, but I knew that's the culture that was prevalent there, not to take responsibility.

So, when you want to be taken seriously, try to be a person of integrity. Don't be pressured to be the same as others. Take responsibility when you are wrong, own up to your mistakes, and speak words where you can back them up 100 times without any letter changing when called upon later to repeat.

Most historical figures who fought for others' rights and freedom, were people of integrity; people who could say to you 'good morning', and you wouldn't need to check your wristwatch to see if it's indeed morning.

Hard work: One of the causes of a negative culture in most workplaces is laziness. A lazy person who wants promotion but knows they don't possess the right work ethics, skills or qualifications to be promoted, tends to then start sucking-up to bosses or management. Such people wouldn't fight for anyone else, because they do not have the right reputation to do so. A person with negative work ethics or who is lazy is like someone whose hands are dirty. If their hands are dirty, they can't engage in any fight for positive change, because they can't stand on that moral podium to fight against injustice or fight for change.

Hard work means doing what is expected of you and if possible, doing extra. Hard work means you are up to date with all tasks required of you that you need to complete. Hard work also means diligence. When people know you are hardworking, you tend to have a better reputation among colleagues, and when you speak, your words tend to carry weight because they're backed up by your reputation as a hardworking person.

Reliability: Being reliable means being consistently good in your performance, and able to be trusted with the responsibilities you take on. It takes time for people to know if you can be trusted and if they can rely on you. So, 'consistency' is the key here. Great sports teams and personalities did not produce just one good result and went off to bed, but they were able to produce great results over and over again, winning trophies and titles consistently within a specific period of time.

Take, for example, Roger Federer, one of the greatest sporting talents of all time. Federer has won a great number of ATP single titles and Grand Slams in his playing career, and you can agree with me that he has been consistent in his winnings.

So being reliable means you are a winner. Workmates tend to trust you more and when you speak, people do listen because your worth is displayed through your consistency, making you an asset to your employer.

<u>Patience</u>: Patience is one of the most important qualities to possess when desiring to fight for change, because if you are not patient enough you could end up ruining a good fight you are supposed to win, ending up losing instead.

Would you agree with me that it is easier to see others faults than our own, especially of those above us? Hence the need for being patient. Patience requires you to examine yourself and see that you don't have any dirt on you before trying to remove others dirt. Patience requires that you try to understand the negative situation. How long has it been going on? Has someone done something about it, and what was the outcome?

Patience requires you to consult with a wide range of other employees to see if they share similar views to you. Patience requires knowing who will back me up when I present my case/arguments for change. Patience requires asking is it the right time to fight this fight? Patience requires asking have I got enough evidence and facts to back me in my fight for change?

Patience is crucial. How long have you been at that workplace? Have you proven yourself at work positively? I will say patience is a great key and you must possess it and use it wisely before you will succeed in your fight for change.

<u>Right timing</u>: Timing is very important. Timing and patience work hand in hand. They sometimes may look the same but they are not. Patience as a quality is gained over time and through experience. And through patience, you will understand timing, and when the time is right to act.

Equally, over the course of time and through experience, you acquire patience. Timing means you have to know when it is the perfect time to fight or advocate for change. If the time is not right for the fight you will fight and lose.

Take, for example, a 10-year-old trying to fight a 22-year-old bully. It's almost impossible due to their physical build, age and fighting skills which are acquired over time. But when that 10-year-old turns 20, and the bully is now in their 30s, the person being bullied most probably has been patient enough to have grown up. Aged 20, he stands a better chance of fighting the bully and succeeding than when he was 10 years old. So, you see he was patient enough to wait to be 20, and it was the probably the right time to stop the bully because he's now more mature now and at a right reasonable age for him to be taking seriously. When he says 'enough', the bully is now more likely to listen.

<u>Respect</u>: I have dedicated a whole lot to talking about respect, so I won't say too much about this great quality here.

But I'd like to point out that respect, whether it's for others or for yourself, is treating others right and as you would want to be treated. Knowing when to speak and when to stay silent. Respecting others is very important, so have respect for all your co-workers and especially your superiors. You may be better or smarter than them but know that you're respecting the position they occupy and the job they do.

Once you are respectful towards others, you too will be viewed positively. People will take you more seriously and your words will reverberate when you speak to others.

The above are not the only qualities to possess to be able to call or advocate for change and have a positive work environment, but they are some of the key attributes to possess or develop, to prepare you for wanting to fight for others and fight for change.

Remember, I am not advocating for violence or confrontation at work. Be careful not to go fighting for change and end up being a bully yourself. You must engage in this fight with empathy for all involved. Your ultimate goal should not be about yourself, but about other employees who can't speak up due to fear or other reasons. It could be for the benefit of future employees who haven't even started working there yet, because you are trying to see that all employees are fairly treated and know that a positive workplace is good for everyone. When positive change occurs, it enhances productivity. It improves work-life balance and your employers, clients and customers will benefit a great deal from it.

Before I finish this chapter, I will share with you a story that happened at a place I once worked. I met Jeff (not real name) who was very hardworking, though a quiet person by nature. He does his work and goes home. I realised Jeff had been working for this security company for about 4 years before I joined, and he's been moved from one site to the other. He was still a casual and at the site I met him on, despite having been there for over 2 years or more. But each time there was an opportunity for promotion he's always overlooked, even though he often performs the acting manager's roles each time the manager is not around.

At a point, he was given the assistant managers role, and then later removed without being told the reasons why. His position was given to another person who could barely write an incident report, and who wasn't even on-site for another four months. But he got the position because that person was close to one of the top bosses.

You see Jeff was a guy who never sucks-up. He does his job, does it very well and goes home. Fast-forward a few months later, instead of the usual two assistant managers, the site will now be having four assistant managers. Yours truly was also chosen among the four. A recently new capable guard to the site was picked, another good guard was chosen, and then management also decided to pick someone who is not capable and, as I said earlier, the same individual who struggled to write emails or reports.

All four of us got a reasonable pay increase, and I mean a good amount with this promotion. But Jeff was never promoted even though he's got a large amount of experience and has been in the industry longer than most of us who were promoted. Why? Because he was a quiet person, didn't suck-up, or was not in the boss's close inner circle. Mind you I don't suck up either, or try to be in the boss's inner caucus. I work hard for my worth.

I went home excited about the recognition I got through the promotion and pay increase! But then I sat down and I realised something is not right here. Jeff is as hardworking as all of us, if not more. He's been consistent and even better than some of us that were promoted, so why wasn't he promoted too?

The next day I went to work and I told my boss and another manager, I am not interested in the position anymore. They asked me why and I said, "Jeff is more qualified and experienced than the four of us that were promoted". If he doesn't get promoted, then I am not good enough for that position. Then one other person declined the promotion also for personal reasons. Take note, I was just part-time and with this promotion, I would be made a full-time employee.

The manager came and had a chat with me and said the other guard (who hasn't got the necessary skills to be an assistant manager) was a management requirement, so I should accept my promotion and let's move on. I declined. She told me I will be moved out of that site if I don't accept. I said well I am fine with that.

A few days later, I was told Jeff would be made one of the assistants, as one of us had declined the position. Jeff would also be made a full-time employee from a casual. I was asked if that was all good with me and if I am happy to still accept the position and I said yes.

The moral of the story is, don't always think about yourself. Stand up for those who can't speak up. There may be consequences but you will always be at peace with yourself and what you stand for.

EXTRA TIP

<u>Join a union</u>: I would always encourage employees to be united within a group or join a government recognised workers union. There are a lot of dodgy operators in the security industry, and the moment you speak for your rights, you either get bullied, threatened or outright experience job loss.

I am an employer today, but I would encourage employees to join a Union. It could help you fight against underpayment, questionable practices, and unreasonable demands by bosses or operators.

I would also encourage other employees who don't have the courage to speak up, to always try and support others who are standing up for them, especially when you are called to support or corroborate events or situation your other colleague is speaking up for, and you know they are telling the truth.

STORY
Threatened, but I Wouldn't Back Down

These are some of the moments you never want to experience at work. Days where someone comes and makes a threat to your life.

The male in question was known to me and to the other security officers. I was phoned and informed he just stole some perfumes. On being questioned by the retail store staff, he gave some back; however, they believed he still had other perfumes with him.

I went after him, but after I'd had a chat with him, he still wouldn't give the rest of the items back. As expected, he was also being rude to me. He was known as someone who each time he walks into the centre he steals or attempts to steal; alcohol, perfume, clothes and what have you.

Yes, there are people like that. We know them and they know we always monitor them or evict them as soon as they walk into the centre. Each time they enter the centre or retail store they are most likely going to steal or the retailer will incur some loss due to their sticky-fingers. That's why the securityofficers are employed, to reduce such loss for the retailers/clients.

So I asked the offending male to leave the centre since he would not give back the rest of the stolen items he still had with him. I told him, "from today, each time you walk into the centre we will ask you to leave". He said, "fine, I will leave," while walking towards the exit. One of the statements he said to me was, "I know your face and I will call my uncle to come and harm you". Well, I wasn't afraid of his threats, but I never take people's threats lightly either.

After he left the centre I rang the police and reported the threats to them. They were going to charge him for the threats he had made to me.

A FEW WEEKS LATER

I was returning from a major first aid incident with two other security officers when I suddenly noticed the same male with his dreadlocks. The moment he saw me he ran into a retailer's store. I decided to go after him to evict him from the centre and I entered the store. I saw him acting like he was on his phone, then I realised he had a pair of brand new jeans he was trying to conceal in his shirt. I knew they were stolen from his body language, but he said no they were his and not a stolen item. I asked for the receipt and he said, "they're my friend's, wait I will call him," but I took the jeans off him and evicted him from the centre and returned the item to the retail store that owned it.

A FEW DAYS LATER AGAIN

I was roving around the centre when I saw someone that looked like 'my dreadlock friend' walking into another retail store. He didn't see me this time, so I walked in, he had another friend with him. I realised 'my sticky-fingered friend' already had a t-shirt in his hands and was trying to tuck it under his shirt. The moment he saw me he turned facing his friend pretending to be talking to him and returned the shirt in his hands onto the clothing hanger it had come off.

His accomplice had a Collingwood Football Club frame in his hands. I knew they had stolen it from the football memorabilia store. The friend's body language gave him away. I asked both of them a few questions and they gave me conflicting answers. Then I ascertained they had stolen the frame and so I evicted both of them from the centre and took the stolen frame back to the retailer that it belonged to.

THINGS I LEARNT

Never take any threat for granted. Always report it and let the police know about it. Try as much as possible not to let it affect how you do your job. Every vocation in life has its dangers, but the love and passion you have for your job will make you face those threats and fears face on.

STORY
Phoney Homeless and Liquor

I have seen a lot of stuff that has made me wiser and somewhat suspicious of certain people because daily I deal with characters who are unpredictable. Then they become predictable because seeing things over and over again makes you have a better understanding of humans and their many ways!

Empathy is very important to have as a person. And as a security officer, it's good to have large amounts of empathy because it does help you deal with so many bad situations and with people of terrible character. Empathy helps you to look at these people through their own life-lenses.

Homelessness is a situation everyone wants to see the end of in our various communities, cities and countries. And yet as our cities become richer and our countries become more advanced and sophisticated, so has the issue of homelessness increased and continued to exist.

I have been homeless on a few occasions in my life. The first I can remember was when my dad and mum separated. I was about 4 to 5 years old back in my home country. I remember my mum and my three other brothers sleeping beneath a stairwell in a strange city that we were later to call our home. I had no idea at that point what we were doing there, but I knew my dear mum was looking for a better place for us.

I understand what it means to be homeless and I do have great empathy for people who are going through homelessness whenever I come across them!

But what about those that take advantage of others by claiming to be homeless when they are not?

Welcome to what happens in our city. Here we have groups of people who come into town wearing dirty clothes, with a handwritten sign with some heart-wrenching description of their plight on a piece of cardboard, holding it with a piety mask on their face. People come dropping money into their bowl because they believe they are helping the homeless.

One day this mum and her little son parked their car and said, "Sir, where is that homeless man that was sitting here a few minutes ago?" She told me, "my son wants to give him some assistance and likes helping the homeless". I said I was sorry but that I had kicked him out because that man is not homeless but a businessman. He parks his car in the rear of the car park and wears dirty clothes and pretends to be homeless to trick people out of their hard-earned money.

They were shocked to hear that! I told her I knew his car and that we had cameras to prove it. I told her of a few others who usually came and sat at the entry of the centre using similar tactics. Some of their friends drop them off in their car and pick them up a few hours later once they make enough money. But before going home they walk straight to the liquor store inside the centre and buy alcohol.

One thing you should understand is, these are organised con-artists pretending to be homeless. The security officer knows them and with video evidence, we daily kick them out of the centre and on a few occasions, they become really aggressive and start swearing at us.

There are heaps of genuine homeless people around who need help and support, but sadly a few people are just ruining it for others. Because they have issues with alcohol and substance abuse, they disguise as homeless people to trick innocent passers-by.

STORY
Homeless and the Blanket

The wisdom of giving is that when you give from the little you have to a person, you should never expect to get anything in return. Most likely you will never get to meet them again, but nevertheless, give with love abounding in your heart. I believe humanity should learn to give such a way.

As a security officer, people often think we are one tough individual with no empathy in our heart, just looking for an opportunity to bully or kick people out of business premises. That is very far from the truth.

The great majority of security officers are regular and loving individuals. They are just doing their job of protecting and maintaining a secure and peaceful atmosphere at their current site/environment.

I remember this one night, it was a weekend. I had just completed my shift at around midnight. I was checking the site perimeters to make sure that everything was okay. After that, I was going to sign off and go home. I was still doing the checks when I saw this homeless man, perhaps he wasn't feeling okay, but it was a very cold night and he had nothing to cover him as he lay there sleeping on the floor. I only had about $21 left in my account, but I felt this man could freeze there before daybreak. I decided to drive about 4 km down the road to a 24/7 store and get a warm fleece blanket. I returned and found the man still sleeping there. I covered him with the blanket and left.

The fleece blanket cost about $15 but I wasn't bothered about the cost. I was more concerned about the homeless man freezing. I felt much better knowing I will sleep tonight in my warm doona, relaxed and feeling confident the homeless man sleeping outside my work is also much warmer and perhaps have a better sleep too!

STORY
Confronted by Mr Muscle

Here comes a man who is covered with muscle on every inch of his body. He's so muscular you might think he invented dumbbells, but this time he's only in the centre to order a milkshake from the juice bar.

I was phoned because the store attendant called the customer name several times when his shake was ready for pick-up, but he never came forward for it. When he later did, he became aggressive and when the female staff tried to speak to him, he just picked up the cup and use it as a projectile to throw at the poor girl!

It's an incident of assault, so I had to discreetly follow the offending male and get his car registration to pass on to the police. Somehow, he noticed I was following him, he came right up to my face and said, "can you tell me what you are doing in the car park?" I replied, "I am doing my job". He was unhappy with my reply and started saying a lot of stuff trying to intimidate and bully me. Then he got to a point where he racially abused me, asking me to return to my country. Mind you this same male is an immigrant. I was upset by his remarks and my response to him was not the best, but it was controlled.

LESSON TO LEARN

I have dealt with a lot of offenders at my place of work and a minute few tend to use racial slurs to deflect from their offence or try to get you to react in a way that will make you look like the aggressor or offending party. From experience, I have learnt to have a thick skin, stay professional and never let the offender's words cause offence to me personally.

Chapter Nine

DISPUTE RESOLUTION

Someone once told me 'there are two parties to an issue and listening to both sides is a valuable exercise'. Humans right from the beginning of history have always been embroiled in disputes. Whether it is as individuals, family units, communities or even countries; conflict has been part of humanity's greatest stories and histories.

Many of these disputes get settled within the bedroom as husband and wife or within the home as a family; others get to the courts and others end up in wars settled by the power of the guns, planes and tanks, etc.

As a security officer, you are a person that has been entrusted by the client not only to keep their property and business secure, but you are also entrusted with some basic authority to settle certain disputes, for example, customer vs store disputes. Some of the other disputes you face will be internal between officers. I will talk about both external and internal disputes.

EXTERNAL DISPUTES

Depending on the site, you will be confronted with so many of these disputes. Sometimes several in a week. Officers that work in retail, events, nightclubs and hospitals tend to have more than their fair share of being confronted with such disputes daily. Some of these disputes could be between patrons.

Example: Daniella was in the nightclub dancing when she reported her ex Giovanni to the bouncer for harassment and intimidation. She made a report three times and he was approached by the bouncer. Giovanni denied all the accusations by his ex, ending up in an argument with the bouncer before getting kicked out of the nightclub.

What Next?: You see the real story is Daniella got jealous seeing her ex Giovanni dancing with another beautiful woman in the club. She made up stories to the bouncer to humiliate her ex and get him kicked out. As a security professional, approach both parties with an open mind. Sometimes the individual who is not telling the truth may look more dramatic than the innocent, so reaching a verdict based on one person's word, emotions and theatrics is dangerous. Approach both individuals with an open mind and listen to both sides of the story. If there are any witnesses, interview them and get their side of their stories too. Where possible and available check your CCTV footage to be certain what went on before any action is taken.

Example (true story): A retailer called security to say that a group of girls, of a different race from the retailer, are being aggressive towards him. I went there with two other officers. I was duty supervisor and the retailer told me the girls stole from him and are unruly and intimidating him. The girls indeed looked aggressive and not in a good mood when we arrived to settle the dispute! Other customers were calling the girls names too and accusing them of what they never saw.

What next: These girls were searched by the retailer and they found no stolen items on them. The girls were followed around the store while they searched for what to buy. The girls asked, "why are you following us?" and they were told, "you girls are being followed because you have stolen from us in the past". Mind you one of the girls just came from interstate and she had proof she doesn't reside locally. I knew the retailer made a false accusation against these girls and I share the same race as one of the accused. I could not tell the retailer he was wrong as I would be perceived to be biased even if the retailer knows he's wrong.

So, I excused myself from settling the dispute and handed the whole situation over to my subordinate who is a first-rate female security officer of Indian origin to deal with it.

The moral of the above examples is that both sides need to be heard before reaching a resolution. If you feel the outcome of your resolution will not be accepted by all parties involved, try to call another workmate to help you. If not, refer the matter to police or management to deal with it.

A lot of patience, listening, wisdom and self-control are always required in every dispute resolution. You may have to encourage both parties to reach a compromise so everyone involved walks away feeling that they've gotten something out of the intervention.

Try not to be part of the problem, stay neutral, remove emotion and handle both parties professionally and fairly. If it happens that there is no other security officer around to assist you, do your utmost to be seen by both parties as being fair. Once again, if you can't reach a resolution get police or management involved.

INTERNAL DISPUTES

I will not say much on this kind of dispute as most workplaces have internal mechanisms for dealing with such disputes, but I will throw in my two cents based on personal and industry experience.

Every officer always wishes they will go to work, complete their job and just come back home happy without being uncomfortable or unhappy in their workplaces. Some of the sources of disputes at the workplace could be an unreasonable boss/superior, a workmate sucking-up to the boss, bullying, sexism, dodgy management practices or outright terrible working conditions. However, whatever is the source of that conflict, I would like you to understand every workplace has theirs. Every security officer will go through at least one conflict with their boss, manager, other security officer or employee in their working life.

ENLIGHTEN YOURSELF

Educate yourself. Try to familiarise yourself with your organisation's conflict resolution mechanism and procedures. Try talking directly and respectfully with the person you are having the conflict with and maybe they can see reason with you. If the matter is not settled, refer the conflict to your supervisor or manager.

Never be quiet about a conflict that has been going on for a long period. Many people quit their jobs or get depressed because of that. Seek help from your boss or manager if talking to the other party doesn't help, or talk to your organisation's human resource department if your supervisor/manager could not reach a resolution.

If you are experiencing depression or suffering as a result of the conflict please seek professional help in the form of counselling or medical treatment.

WHAT IF IT'S YOUR BOSS?

Some supervisors, managers and leaders in the industry tend to act in ways that are unprofessional, with outright bullying or harassment of their staff. Because guards want to keep their jobs and positions, then they end up putting up with a lot of this dirty and terrible behaviour. This should not be so. If you put up with it today it may end up being a pattern and others may suffer from similar negative behaviour after you.

Speak to the boss in person and tell him/her you are not happy with their behaviour. If change doesn't happen, speak to other employees to see if they have experienced similar bad behaviour from the boss or have witnessed such.

Report the boss to any other immediate superior or HR and if nothing is done. Further options could include contacting the union or government ombudsman that deals with workplace conflict or obtain legal advice.

The aim of settling disputes should not be for payback, vengeance or blackmail. It should be to create a conducive and respectful working environment for every security officer regardless of their position, gender or race.

STORY
Who Owns the Fifty Bucks?

Now, this was one of the most hilarious incidents I have witnessed at work!

An officer got called because some customers were arguing over $50. Two women were pushing a shopping-trolley and they suddenly found a $50 note on the floor. An older-looking woman who was coming in the opposite direction at the same time as the women who found the money said to the women as soon as they picked up the $50, "it's my money".

Well, those two women wouldn't buy the story that the $50 belonged to her and perhaps they asked her a few questions and she kept on insisting it's hers. Then it almost escalated into a fight. Security officers intervened and checked the camera and saw that the woman claiming the money was hers never had anything to do with the money but was fighting tooth and nail that it was her $50 and she wanted it!

Chapter Ten

RESPECT FOR ALL EMPLOYEES, CUSTOMERS AND CLIENTS

The security industry is one that will always have jobs available for people; because as the world's population grows and as technology grows, so too does criminal activity grow. Hence the need for more security personnel to secure our communities, businesses and country.

DIVERSE PERSONNEL

As the saying goes, 'respect is reciprocal', and respect is a rare quality every security officer will need in order for them to excel in building lasting, cordial relationships with their colleagues throughout in their career.

Today the world is also known as a global village, because as the world changes, so too are people emigrating from one part of the planet to the other.

The security industry today is not just about the quality of personnel, but also about the availability of people willing to join the industry. As the demand for manpower increases, so too has the industry become more diverse; filled with people from different social and cultural backgrounds.

Not only is the industry saturated with people from different cultural and racial backgrounds (which is good for the industry), it is also not just the industry of the boys' club anymore, but of everyone.

In every given security site or location, you will find all officers employed come from diverse backgrounds. As such, respect for every employee, regardless of where they come from or their gender, should be accorded to everyone.

Security is a team enterprise, and the stronger the unit is the better the security team will perform! The thing that brings people together the most is the respect that they have for each and every one of the team members and for what they each bring to the table.

TRUE STORY

I have worked in a site where a guard (whether you call him old school or not, I know such behaviour does not belong in the 21st century) insinuated that he does not believe a female security officer is capable of being a supervisor. He doesn't believe in a female security officer being in a leadership position. Hence the disrespect he has for a particular female officer, even though she is fantastic at what she does, and is one of the most hardworking and experienced officers on that particular site.

There are those who also think that someone of a different race, cultural or religious background to themselves is not good enough to be the leader of security officers, but that's not true. Experience and capability to do the said task or job should be what is considered and not the officer's background or gender.

WHAT BREEDS NEGATIVE ATTITUDES

I personally believe respect starts when we have self-respect. When you have respect for yourself, others can see it and in turn, you will be respected by others. What about when you have respect for yourself and someone doesn't have respect for you? Well, that person might not have respect for their own self in the first place, and that's why they fail to respect you.

Respect is a culture practised deep within oneself. Respect is a culture practised at home that comes into the workplace with us. Respect or lack of it is a culture practised by the environment that shaped us. So, when you see someone being disrespectful, most likely they've been shaped by their past culture, environment or home. But luckily, such negative culture can be changed.

Our places of work are not just for us to come to, earn money and go home, but are places of learning. A place of influence and a place with its own culture. As a leader in any given place of employment, you must understand that some of your responsibility is to create a positive culture. A culture of respect and integrity within a workplace is best if you are able to inspire every employee to embody such a culture within them.

As every employee that works for you will have the opportunity to learn something new from you and your workplace; will that something new they learn to be positive or negative?

What they learn while under your leadership, they will take with them in their respective life's journey. That will determine if they, in turn, will be of positive or negative influence with the new people they will meet and work with later on.

This applies not just for leaders at workplaces, but for all employees who learn from each other daily. That's why every security officer must learn and practice the culture of respect with their workmates and every human.

The religion, race, gender, social or cultural background of your fellow co-worker doesn't matter. What matters is that everyone deserves to be respected and treated as a valued and equal co-worker.

Respect is also showing love. When you respect others it's a message of love to the other person, and it also shows you to be a person of great maturity. In return, others will give you great respect back!

STORY
Thief Almost Tasered Me

In large shopping centres, Saturdays are always a busy day. It's always packed with families, everyone trying to do their shopping for the coming week and a few others trying to source for an opportunity to steal what they can!

However, the good thing about where I was working was that we have some of the best security officers around. Security guards that have got years of experience, well trained and have great self-control.

BACK TO THE STORY

This day was like all other days, it started very busily early in the morning when we got a call about a well-known offender who had assaulted one of the security officers that works inside a retail store. A few hours later, our control room operator got called about some guy who had just stolen a box of perfume and makeup. I was the duty supervisor so I hurriedly proceeded to the store.

It was a pharmacy. I waited outside to see if the male would walk out of the store without paying, then it would be classified as theft (in Australia). Indeed the man walked out with the items! With one of the pharmacy staff, I requested a bag search. This offender became aggressive, swore at me and claimed he's got nothing on him, even though store employees saw him stealing and CCTV prove that he stole.

Since he declined a bag check and I know he's got the items with him, I asked him to leave the centre. I can't forcefully retrieve the stolen items from him, so I decided to escort him out.

This bloke seemed to be in his mid-fifties, and he had his daughter with him and another lady with a child. I kind of wonder, once again, what kind of dad is this man? What example he is setting for his kids? This fella seems not to care, however, he was feeling embarrassed about being kicked out of the centre. I decided to call the police and report the incident while escorting the male out of the centre.

We got to the car park and suddenly this man, whom I was about 5 inches taller, and much younger and stronger than, decided to start shoving me and punched me in the chest. I kept my cool, continued making the phone call, but this man wouldn't calm down. He became more aggressive and called me all kinds of names, but I understand security so I don't take things personally or try use muscle to settle a score, but instead use my brain. I decided to make an effort to get his car registration so I could pass it to the police because he's not only stolen but assaulted me.

We then got much closer to his vehicle, then all of the sudden this crazy man ran straight into his car and brought out a taser! He was threatening to taser me, with the electric spark zapping! Tasers are illegal to own in Australia for all civilians, so not only had he stolen and assaulted, but he's in possession of an illegal weapon and making further threats! I did laugh, even though this was a tense situation. I only laughed because I got his car registration and am sure the police will book an appointment with him soon, as I passed all the details of this offender to them.

Chapter Eleven

RIGHT ATTITUDE WILL TAKE YOU PLACES

Your brainpower, which includes emotional intelligence (EQ) and social intelligence (SQ), is much more important and effective in the security industry than your physical strength. Brainpower (switched-on, smart, calm in all situations, measured in words) will take you far in the industry and your career, while your physical strength will most likely land you before a magistrate trying to defend your use of force or actions.

I have seen a very young officer, well built and physically strong, whose house was less than a minute walking distance from his place of employment. He loved his security job and was always eager to help out, but his method of applying excessive physical strength to solve conflicts on numerous occasions led to the client not being happy for him to remain onsite. He could get their business taken to court and that could lead to financial loss.

This young officer now had to travel 45 minutes away from his home to get to work in order to find a job more suited to his physical abilities.

I have also met an officer on another job with more than two decades in security who took pride in telling anyone that cared to listen, how long he'd been in the industry. However, within the first few weeks of his employment at that site, people started making complaints against this particular officer. From the casual security guards to other contractors and what have you.

The complaints were simply due to his inability to communicate with people in a calm, respectful and courteous manner. This officer had to be on probation for a period before his employment could confirm him as permanent full-time. Unfortunately, the complaints and drama were so much that a day before his probation finished he was informed he wouldn't be offered a permanent full-time position.

Both cases were unhappy experiences for those involved, but it's good for people to learn that as a security officer a lot of responsibilities are being placed in our care by the client and employer. A client wants to be confident in the knowledge that an officer can be trusted to look after their business. An officer that the client knows will save them money by doing what is legal and right, and not someone who would do anything illegal that might end up costing them money in civil litigation.

That is why every security officer must understand that clients will not accept terrible behaviour, but instead, will reward behaviours and actions that save them money and bring positive feedback and publicity to their businesses.

I know a guy called Joe (not his real name), who was always very respectful to other guards and treated people with respect and dignity. He was just one of four team leaders working with the site supervisor.

He lived far away from work and had a long commute, but he always got the job done. Since I had worked on that site I had never heard anyone make a complaint against Joe.

The site supervisor at that particular site had always given the impression that he wouldn't be there for long. His position appeared to be an attractive one with generous pay and great working hours, so it was definitely a job other officers would eye if such position were to become vacant.

One day the supervisor resigned. There were four team leaders assisting the supervisor and all four were eligible to be made the new site supervisor. Guess who was given the supervisor role? Joe,

I'm pleased to say. He never looked like he'd canvassed or lobbied for the role, but one particular security officer had always coveted the position, and I mean a guard with questionable character and antics.

When I heard Joe was promoted to be the site supervisor I felt the right thing had been done. He deserved the position because he was a person with a great reputation and fantastic work ethic. Joe had never tried to undermine the old supervisor and had always treated him and everyone else with respect.

The moral of the above story is that Joe approached his job with the right attitude and treated others well. He got on with his job and never appeared desperate, but ended up being promoted to a position that many people wanted because he always had a fantastic attitude!

STORY
Arrive Early or Meet Pharrell Williams

I started a job with a new employer and I was really enjoying the events related shifts that were coming my way. This company handled the security for lots of major events, including a variety of international sporting events. It was a great opportunity to gain heaps of on the job experience as I'd only been in the security industry for a year.

I remember I was rostered to start my shift around 10.30 a.m. I was on site around 10.15 a.m to sign on. To my surprise, the event manager informed me, "I'm sorry, you are supposed to be on site 30 minutes before your shift!"

I was disappointed and impressed at the same time! I have always had more respect for people who are professional in their approach to work, even though I was disappointed that no one had informed me about this 30 minutes early business.

I took what they told me in good faith and was about to go home, but the events manager said, "just hang on a little bit, although we have assigned someone to your role, the next set of guards starting later, if any of them don't come early, we will give you their shift". This particular event manager was the one who had given me the job through a mutual friend of ours.

I was told hang on, so I had nothing to do but to sit and wait. While I was waiting and thinking of my missed opportunity to make extra $$, the in-house manager that ran the sporting venue came (driving on a 4-wheel quad bike). He rushed into the shed and chatted with our events manager for a few minutes before calling me over. They had found a new role for me.

They had realised there was a need for an extra guard which they had never organised, so I was the perfect candidate; available but with no role yet.

I was told to join the in-house manager on his quad. He drove very fast back to the main stand that also had a Members Only area. The occasion today was not sports but a massive summer music festival.

I was taken into an elevator to the top level of the Members Only section. I then got introduced to a muscular looking African-American guy. He welcomed me and said, "I'm head bodyguard for Pharrell Williams. Your job is to be at the entry door and look after his family while he's on stage. He's going to be performing today and if you need anything let us know".

I was stunned! The members only section had an apartment where Pharrell, his family and entourage were staying and my task was to be at the door of the living room. I loved my new responsibility and I kind of felt rewarded for having not arrived on time.

Chapter Twelve

PRESENTATION, EXERCISE, PERSONAL HYGIENE

STORY

I saw the security officer looking at his wristwatch on his hand before saying, "I did 40 kilometres today." I realised it was a Fit Bit and he's working at one of the world's biggest stadiums on a 12-hour shift. He had about four hours more to go when he mentioned 40 km. Yes, that's a true story. Many officers cover more than 40 km of walking in a single shift, depending on the site.

Security guards for both retail and events do a lot of walking in a single shift. Static guards do a lot of standing and control room officers tend to be seated, but no matter what role you are doing in the industry, I would always encourage officers to look after their health and have a reasonable amount of fitness.

<u>Exercise</u>: The security industry is primarily focused on customer service, but next to that comes 'presence'. By this, I mean that often times your presence could deter an offender from wanting to commit a criminal act by merely looking at you.

So, it is important to look after your health and to try as much as you can to keep fit. You could be required to help emergency services lift a patron they're attending to or a customer who may require your assistance in helping them walk or be on their feet.

Going to the gym is a great way to keep fit, build your confidence and be in good general health. It will help you build up more strength to assist customers and others when strength is required, as well as giving you a very positive presence too. Don't go to the gym because you want to build muscle to fight patrons or you want to look macho. If that's your aim then you may end up attracting patrons who would bait you into a fight or conflict.

<u>Health</u>: Keep in tune with your body and make sure you are in the best shape possible. Don't overwork yourself just because you want to earn more money. Your health may end up paying for it when really, your health should be your top most priority.

<u>Dress well</u>: People will often address you the way you dress. People tend to have more respect and courtesy for people who really dress well. You tend to look more approachable and worthy of respect when you dress well because you represent class or should I say your dress makes sense!

Being a security officer does not mean you dress badly. You portray the image you want to be seen, so you must always dress smart, clean and professional.

Wearing worn-out clothes and shoes won't do it. You want to be respected and taken seriously, don't you? Then dress well and appropriately.

<u>Grooming & personal hygiene</u>: You are a security officer and not a gangster. I hope I don't appear like I am making a judgement but you are not here to represent yourself or your ideas. Rather, you represent the client/employer to the customer, therefore good personal hygiene is essential.

Most employers will require all officers to be well-groomed and their hair and beards neatly shaved and trimmed. Likewise, some of us, due to what we eat (e.g spicy food) are prone to sweating a lot. Strong body odours can be kept in check with just a $3 roll-on deodorant applied regularly. We need to keep an eye on our diets too so we don't go to work and make others uncomfortable due to an undesirable odour.

I know it's a hard topic to talk about, but I'd like to talk about it in this book so that any officer who may be having challenges with their breath, body odour or any other personal hygiene issue does not ignore it, but seeks the necessary help so that they can do their job more confidently.

I would also encourage workmates to be patient with the employee who may be experiencing issues with their personal hygiene. Don't make fun of the afflicted officer or give them an inhumane nickname, but show them love and if you can, privately speak to them about it and if possible offer them help.

Safety: Always follow your organisations OH&S safety procedures. They were designed to keep you, patrons, contractors and every employee safe and the opportunity to carry out their duties in a safe working environment.

Before you do your job or task, always make sure you assess your working environment and the task you would be undertaking to check if it is a safe environment or a safe job to do.

If in doubt of your or others safety, immediately stop the job, and if possible isolate the area and report it to your immediate superior or your health and safety representative.

STORY
Stole, Eating with Family After

It was Saturday afternoon; the weather was sunny and everyone was enjoying the serene shopping and dining atmosphere at my workplace. As a security officer, I was just doing what I love doing, roving in the centre until my supervisor got this call from one of the retail stores; a family had just stolen sunglasses from their store.

My supervisor is pretty good on the CCTV and I mean really good! He went straight to action. All officers were informed of the theft and our duty manager was on the lookout too. My supervisor managed to track the well-dressed male with his wife and little child (about 6 or 7years old) and found them eating in the food court area.

My supervisor did a further review of the cameras and discovered the culprits had dispatched the stolen sunnies into their car with their other shopping bags before the whole family returned to the centre to enjoy the beautiful ambience of the food court and the great tasty meals on offer. Did I tell you the restaurants in the shopping centre have some of the tastiest food on offer in Melbourne?

Police were notified and my supervisor did a further review of the family movements in the centre and discovered they had been into multiple stores and stolen as much as they could.

Now this family had a very expensive car, was well-dressed and sleek, also they used their child to distract retailers before they stole. Sadly, I have seen lots of adults train and use little kids to steal!

It's such a sad thing to see parents who have been blessed with children, start teaching them how to do the wrong thing from an early age.

Police arrived and arrested the father who was very much the ringleader. They searched the family's vehicle and found stolen items worth more than $3000 taken from multiple stores.

So, you can see how a report of the theft of just a single pair of sunglasses led to something much bigger.

Chapter Thirteen

SHIFT WORK AND NIGHT SHIFTS

This chapter on shift work is a very important subject to me. Like other chapters I have written so far, this particular chapter is dear to me because I went through the experience personally and it wasn't a pleasant one.

Over the years, I have worked in so many security jobs and on different sites. Some of the jobs I did were day shifts, afternoon shifts and night shifts. I can tell you, I was fortunate to learn what is best for my body and mental wellbeing. I hope what I will share here will be of great benefit to you as well.

Have you done night shifts of around 12 hours per shift and worked three 12-hour shifts in a row? Then you come back home after the third shift and your partner or friend tries to get you to do some chores or to go out someplace. Your reaction was just moody or your reply was a bit unpleasant and they ask what's wrong with you or why are you not helping enough?

Perhaps your circadian rhythm is being affected by the kind of shifts you do and you feel lethargic, and in a way, lacking control.

Your mental health is very important in order for you to function properly and effectively at work and at home. You must find the right balance and what kind of shift and hours of work suits you as a person.

DAY, AFTERNOON AND NIGHT

A good amount of people in the industry only focus on the dollars. As long as they can get a lot of hours to work, then they are willing to do it. Some officers also feel the need to do a lot of long, continuous shifts and longer hours because they want to buy a house or go on a holiday or they just want to make as much money as possible to retire early.

What is the point of buying a house if you have bad mental health, going on a holiday depressed, or saving enough for early retirement only to suffer from bad health that won't let you enjoy your retirement?

To some security officers, whether it's day, afternoon or night shift, they cope exceedingly well and it doesn't affect them in any way. While others can only cope with day shifts or afternoon shifts. A small minority I have met prefer night shifts only and they manage well doing such shifts.

It is important as a security officer that you try all shifts for a few weeks or months to determine what is best for you. See if you are able to do all shifts types and still have a great work-life balance or without suffering any health issues like anxiety, depression or mood swings. Trying all kind of shifts will help you determine this and discover what you're best suited for.

Humans are all different and it is important we each understand our bodies and what we are capable of and what is best for us.

If after a few months you're not able to determine what shifts best suits you, perhaps do the shift work for a year or two and then see which shifts affect you negatively or mentally. After you are able to determine which shift is most suitable for you, then make the right decision and only do shifts that you believe best suits you or find a new site or job that can offer such shifts for the sake of your health and loved ones.

Personally, when I work during the day, for example, 7 a.m. to 7 p.m. or afternoon, or say anything from 3 p.m. to midnight, I tend to be fine and have a normal lifestyle. When it's from 7 p.m. to 7 a.m., that is when my health suffers and I become less productive at home and with others.

MY DISCOVERY

When I started working in the security industry, in my first bona fide shift work, I worked different, odd hours. I remember my first security job was an 18th birthday party at Mount Martha in Victoria. I was proud of that job I must confess and it was at the odd hour of the day.

As the weeks and months went by, I kept on doing very odd jobs here and there, and at different hours of the day. It was all fine until I got placed on a permanent site as a reliever; that was to relieve all guards who are going on holidays every month, so that meant I had to cover their rotating roster of two weeks of day shifts and two weeks of night shifts.

I did that job for a few months. When I finished my two or three days straight night shift, I would have two to three days off, but then I discovered something; I found myself always sleeping at odd hours of the day and I became very unhelpful at home. I played less with my kids and my empathy and tolerance level became really low.

I didn't understand what was going on. I also became depressed. Then I went back to drinking alcohol, even though I had quit for almost three years.

Months later, I discovered I was unsuitable for night shifts and it had affected my mental wellbeing. I started drinking, and then I lost my driver's licence after that. I also lost my well-paid job.

One of the things that led me to such a situation, however, was that I was employed on a casual contract so I could hardly turn down the shifts I was given. The problem was not just the night shifts, but being casual, I had to accept and do what was not right for my well-being. I was also naive to the negative effect of night shifts on me.

A few months later, I got another ad-hoc job just a short walking distance from home. It was the perfect job as I had no driver's licence.

I had to impress my new workmates so I could be given a permanent roster. I took every shift that came my way, worked hard and later got given a permanent rotating roster.

I worked really hard and did a lot of excessive shifts. My roster was nights then days and again I got seriously depressed. My marriage was in danger as my ex-wife became unhappy. I didn't help much at home and was always sleeping or drinking. A few months later, I realised I can't continue like this. I told my supervisor that I was quitting my job. The excessive shifts, especially at night, were not good for me. Then I was offered work in one of our sister sites doing afternoon shifts. I loved those shifts but by then trying to quit alcohol had become an uphill task and I was still battling depression and my marriage was crumbling.

What helped me to overcome my depression and bad situation was the ultimate discovery that I am not built for doing night shifts or working excessive amounts of overtime. I was also helped through this period by visits to a GP for mental health support and by my Christian faith.

I decided to stick with day and afternoon shifts, and I quit drinking alcohol. Although my marriage was over, I became a better person and a better father after learning to only accept what's right for me no matter the amount of money or employment I will lose.

MY OBSERVATION

I've worked in so many sites and one thing I've discovered is that a lot of the guards who engage in excessive overtime and night shifts, tend to always be in a bad mood, angry or borderline bullies.

Yes, they make the $$ but they don't often look happy and they tend to have poor work-life balance.

Perhaps people focus more on making money than on their health. Perhaps they fail to know what shift is best suited for them and for their health.

Some officers can attest to that; when they do night shifts their mood at home tends to be really bad. They are more inclined to have conflicts with workmates, contractors or even customers, due to the accumulated stress coming from working night shifts or excessive overtime.

KNOW WHAT'S BEST FOR YOU

A few months later I was promoted at my workplace. My pay got bumped up really well, but the job required I do shift work.

That was a conundrum for me. I worked near home, the pay was good, I liked the people I worked with and I loved my job.

I did the job for about two weeks but sadly I had to resign because I knew I couldn't do night shifts without my health suffering.

I later got my driver's licence back and got my life back, so I quit my high paying job and went for a new job where I worked fewer hours per shift and it was during the day.

I made less money, but I enjoyed the job. Although I travelled 60 km more per shift, I was a better father and person again because I was depression free and my mental health drastically improved.

I said to myself this time without thinking about the sums, money is not everything. Our physical, mental and emotional wellbeing is essential because with good health you will be a better workmate, partner, parent and person in general.

PEOPLE'S BEHAVIOUR

Often when you see people start doing drugs or drinking excessively and you talk to them, you will discover they are going through one personal challenge or another that's affecting their mental health.

Disclaimer: there is no excuse for drink driving or while on drugs, so don't drive when you're under the influence of either.

SEEK HELP

One thing I have observed in the industry is that a lot of officers do night shifts because it's the site's working requirements and they have no option. But I would advise you, if possible, to look for another place of employment or consider a change of career if you feel the entire job on offer requires you to do shift work that will be detrimental to your health.

Your pay may take a nosedive or you may lose friends, but trust me you will keep good health, family and friends.

If you are ever going through any mental or health challenges speak to someone about it. Some workplaces or industries offer mental health support services. Speak to your employer and see how they can assist you if you are going through any stress, anxiety or depression.

You can also contact your local, state or national mental health support service by searching for them online. If you are in Australia, services such as Beyond Blue, Lifeline and Headspace can offer you support.

Also, never be ashamed to speak to your partner, relatives, friends or workmates about your struggle with mental health issues. Fighting it alone is tough, so it's best to fight it with your loved one's support.

Chapter Fourteen

DEALING WITH TRAUMA, INJURIES AND GRIEF AT WORK

Security work is always filled with adventure, drama, excitement and what have you! There are also many layers to the job in security. Most times it's dependent on an officer handling the particular situation, site history and other times just unexpected full-blown drama/adventure.

Some security jobs, depending on the site and type of security, have more safety issues than the others.

Take, for example, security officers working in hospitals dealing with patients that might be affected by prohibited substance or patients who are dealing with psychological/mental challenges. Such kind of security work tends to have security officers experiencing more adventure, safety concerns and possible harm than a guard whose single job is to sit in a patrol vehicle watching a construction site or a guard in a gatehouse.

I am sure officers working in cash delivery businesses, nightclubs, shopping centres and many other examples are likely to dispute that their type of security is more open to danger than others. The point is not to stoke argument but to point out that security officers are a very brave set of people who face daily challenges and dangers that are unimaginable. However, because of the love of the job and other factors, they soldier on, providing safety and customer service for the patrons, clients and various communities. I say well done to every person that is involved in the business of security!

INJURIES, TRAUMA AND DANGERS

It's of great importance for all security professionals to regularly go through health and safety training. Indeed, there are a lot of reputable security companies that train their employees periodically or annually on health and safety and other sorts of training to improve their officer's service delivery.

The officer must understand that they are expected by their families, friends and employer to go to work and come back home safe and happy.

Your health and safety at work and that of others are very important. It is good to always be aware of your work environment as to be sure that it's a safe place to work for yourself and your work colleagues. If you have any safety concerns while at your work you should feel free to contact your in-house safety officer or supervisor/manager and report such concerns or observations.

Our focus should not only be on physical health and safety alone but also unseen or silent areas of our health such as mental health and how to maintain work-life balance and not put too much pressure on oneself or turn the workplace into a stressful environment. What about the things that happen at work that could inflict trauma on the guard? These are areas of health and safety we must keep an eye on and also discuss.

We are indeed all different and all of us deal with trauma, threats and dangers in differing ways. It is important they are well dealt with, so never be ashamed to share with someone what you are going through or to seek professional help.

Don't try to be a hero security officer. Try and be professional at all times and follow your site-specific health and safety procedures.

DEALINGS

Injury: When injured at work, seek medical attention and also report such injury to your employer. Do not force yourself to work or allow the employer to force you to work while still injured. Your health is very important. The healthier you are, the more you're able to work and earn a living.

If you discover your injury is serious while seeking medical attention and it will affect your ability to work for a long time, communicate with your employer and see how you can get some form of Work cover or workers compensation. Take note: this could also negatively affect your future employment prospects, so be honest and only go for such compensation when you know you're telling the truth and you think it's indeed necessary.

Trauma: A lot of security officers experience work-related trauma. It could be as a result of what they have witnessed, experienced or actions of others towards them. Get in touch with your employer's HR department if your supervisor/manager can't help. I would also advise you to seek professional help if possible.

Do not force yourself to keep working when you're experiencing trauma, as your productivity is likely to be low and it could affect you and your other workmates.

Grief: This is a subject that most people never like to discuss, but I feel there are a few things to be learnt from such dark moments that we all face at some point in life, whether at work or at home.

As a security officer, when such dark moments at work come, how do we deal with it, how do we get past it and how do we come out stronger?

I have worked in a security environment where the guards or I have seen people, sadly, pass away! For the sake of the family and respect of those that pass, I won't elaborate more on such a sad workplace event.

I will talk about how you can deal with such a sad experience. Whether it's a co-worker or a patron, people we know or just visitors that passed by, one thing I know is that at the end of the day we are humans and we have that emotional side of us that gets touched by what we have just witnessed.

We are all different and are most likely to deal with things differently, but take this message with you, such dark experiences are not unique to one workplace or to you alone. Others have dealt with similar experiences. It's not your fault and you only happened to be there when such an event happened.

When I say dark experience, it's not limited to witnessing someone passing away at work, but it could be seeing a very terrible injury or witnessing a brutal fight, etc. Often such an experience leaves the officer feeling traumatised. Others may end up quitting their jobs or going on extended leave.

Whatever it is that you have experienced or witnessed, don't be ashamed to speak up, ask for help or take time off work. If that's what would help to make you feel better then go for it. But never be ashamed to seek help, is what I would advise.

STORY
Stabbed with Screwdriver

A job you do but that you never enjoy, it's best you quit and go fishing or do something else.

I take delight in doing my job as a security officer. It kind of makes me feel I am not just working for money, but serving others and my community.

Each time I get called for a theft or any incident, I take pleasure in trying to ensure that the retailer, client or customer gets their item back so that there is a positive outcome from my intervention and peace is restored to the situation.

This particular day, I was informed a male had just stolen a number of items from a major clothing store in the centre. My site supervisor who was operating the cameras was monitoring the offender, while the store manager and I were heading towards the current location of the offender.

The manager and I were informed that the offender was inside a supermarket. We also received a physical description of the offender.

I walked up to the male and courteously said to him, "the manager of the clothing store you just left would like to do a bag-check with you if that's okay". Before I could finish making that statement and point to the manager who stood right behind me, the male, who was on methamphetamine (ice) or some other kind of illegal drug brought out a screwdriver to stab me. I wasn't able to run away because I was too close to the offender and my survival instinct kicked in. I had to protect myself by holding his hands with the screwdriver in them. We both struggled a bit and I overpowered him and took the screwdriver out of his hands.

I restrained him to the floor, while backup was called. A few seconds later one of the supermarket staff that was brave enough came and assisted me in restraining the male, as the offender was on drugs, I needed as much help as I could get.

A few minutes later police arrived, the stolen items were recovered and the male was arrested. I went straight to the medical centre and got an anti-tetanus injection because I had received a slight cut. I completed my shift and took two days sick leave because the injection I was given wouldn't let me function properly and affected my mobility.

ADVICE NOT TO TAKE

I had some advice from a few people to take workers compensation, etc., but I rejected such advice because I am very principled. I love my job and I believe that's not the right thing to do since I would be able to return to work in just a few short days.

I am not trying to say don't take Workcover if you have a genuine reason to, but I am saying don't just be hoping for every opportunity that comes your way or view Workcover as though it's a lottery. Sometimes Workcover is a debt that you pay back later when future employers only give you a job as a casual because they are scared you will claim workers compensation a lot! If you're thinking of full-time employment with a new employer after you have accessed Workcover, I think it would be far more difficult after the fact.

Chapter Fifteen

RETAIL AND SECURITY

I'm sure a lot of people have watched the movie *Mall Cop*. It's a film that sheds a bit of light about the security officer, what they go through and the sorts of things they face at work.

Although it only showed a small portion of what the officer goes through, and all retail outlets are different, most officers share a somewhat similar experience. Also, keep in mind that the majority of retail security officers are not people who tried to join the police force and failed. Nevertheless, I have come across several security guards' who after being a security officer have been inspired to want to join the police force.

According to the Australian Retailers Association, theft costs local retailers approximately $7.5 billion per year (www.retail.org.au), hence the need for retailers to be investing more in security and loss prevention personnel.

As you have seen in this book, a lot of the stories were from within a retail environment and all are true stories. These experiences led me to the conclusion that I really needed to write something that could help the security and loss prevention officer take their game to the next level and also help the retail employee to understand what they are dealing with and how best to approach these situations.

Take note, what I am writing does not claim to show you every trick of the intending offender, but rather, serves as a guide to help you be more alert and proactive towards securing your business.

Retail staff: I have worked with a lot of retail staff and employees who run or manage a retail store and many of them are fantastic people who know what they are doing and love what they do!

I have come to realise that while some retailers are very good at their jobs, when it comes to security and managing theft and loss prevention they often struggle with it. They don't know how to deal with such situations.

I hope through my own experience that I will be able to shed some light on this area which may be of some help to retailers.

THINGS TO CONSIDER

Environment: It is imperative to understand the community and demographic of your store or shopping centre is based in. Where it is located affects the patronage and will help you a lot in understanding the kind of customers that will be shopping in your business.

Once you understand your environment, this will also assist you in making better security decisions for your business. Like, what kind of security will be required based on the patrons that are most likely to walk in?

History: Research your store or shopping centre's past. It could be by asking the centre's securityguards, centre management, nearby stores or even by reading some news articles online. See if there have been any major security issues in the past or incidents that could help you make the most fitting security arrangements for your business or store; especially in relation to stock, exit and entry points for patrons.

Customers: You know your store and often you may think you know your customers, but that's not always true. Yes, all customers may likely spend money at your business, but don't judge a book by its cover.

<u>True story</u>: The story previously mentioned in this book, the customer who walked into the centre with his wife and two kids, all well dressed in expensive clothing looking really slick and rich, and proceed to go into several stores and steal items worth almost $3,000. How could they have done that? Often the retailer sees someone wearing expensive and good-looking clothes and they tend to let their guard down. They think it's some kind of wealthy big shot; but no, those fancy clothes are just a shoplifting costume.

While you are focused on the scruffy looking and unkempt patron, the well-dressed patron will raid your store/stock and leave you smiling with their Gucci perfume smell in your store!

Be open-minded and treat every patron the same. They could be genuine customers or they could touch your stock and it would disappear.

A lot of times the customers who are the friendliest to you are actually being friendly to win your trust and make you feel comfortable with them before they steal your stock.

Be professionally open-minded and don't let their smiles, how good looking or well-dressed they are to distract you. Be friendly, but always be alert and keep your eyes open.

<u>Liaise with centre security</u>: If you operate in a shopping centre or some kind of environment that has security personnel, get to know the security manager/supervisor and have regular interaction with all the security officers.

Make sure you have their phone number so that you can call them anytime you require assistance.

Hold periodic meetings with them and enquire after their operational procedures for assisting retailers. Ask them how they think you can improve your security and minimise stock theft.

Be friendly with the security officers and they will always make your security their priority, assisting you swiftly every time you call them.

Liaise with police: Yes, your local police are very important for your business security. It's essential you know your local police programme for assisting businesses.

Always inform them of any theft or incident that happens in your store. It may only be a minor one, but getting the police involved could lead to an offender being arrested for another bigger crime they previously committed or are planning to commit.

Your own security: There are lots of security companies who can help you do a risk assessment for your business. They can tell you how to improve the security of your stock and personnel. They can recommend what type of security services you may need, such as loss prevention officers, security cameras and access control, etc.

Dealing with incidents: It's important to understand beforehand what the store or centre procedures are for dealing with incidents or reporting incidents to security or police.

If you arm yourself with such procedural knowledge, you are more likely to recover stolen goods and have the offenders arrested and prosecuted.

Most of the times retailers fail to report incidents to security or police because they feel it's just a very minor theft or that nothing can be done about it.

On several occasions, I have seen patrons who stole just one small item, security was called and police were notified. The offender was arrested as a result of centre security tracking offenders and obtaining their vehicle number plates. Often such offenders have committed other major crimes and police have been on the lookout for them. With the help of the retailer and security, this offender has subsequently been arrested and they are off our streets for good!

SIMPLE STEPS TO FOLLOW

In-store cameras: I would always advise retail stores to have in-store cameras. They can be used by retailers both to monitor suspicious customers in real-time and by review. Showing exactly what the offender was doing in the store, which can then also be used as evidence with incidents that may end up going to court.

Extra staff: It is always advisable to have at least two staff at your store, especially during busy hours or days. Most shoplifters or troublemakers tend to target stores that have only one staff member on the floor as they often operate in groups, where one person distracts the staff member while the other steals from the store.

Centre security guards ask store staff members to accompany them when they are after suspected shoplifters. The store staff can help to identify the right person and ask for the items back, all the while security is there to back them up. It may seem strange that security guards can't go alone and retrieve items without a staff member with them, however, it is important that the person approaching the offender must have witnessed the crime that was committed, in most cases the witness is the retailer and the security officer would only act as a back-up to the retailer to retrieve their items.

In the event the security officer approaches the customer/suspect without being a witness, the customer whom the security guard is after could sue the security officer or their employer. If the security officer is without any physical, pictorial or video evidence approaches the customer and asks them about a purported stolen item when in reality they are innocent. That would be defamation. Therefore, it is important that an extra staff member comes along with the security officer when going after an offender. The staff must have witnessed the crime and be 100% sure that the customer you are going after is the correct one and has been seen committing the offence.

Call security: As soon as an offence is committed in your store, call security straight away. If there is any CCTV footage, forward it to the officer's phone and give the security guard a description of what the offender looks like. This way they can track them and then call you to assist them with going after the offender.

Call the police: After an incident is reported to security, call the police and report the said incident to them, so they are aware of it and can come to assist you.

Retail security: Retail security and loss prevention is a job some security guards don't want to do and they run away from. There are many reasons why they do so and I will list a few.

A FEW REASONS WHY

Walking: I am sure you have been to a few shopping centres and you've seen the security officer walking around smiling and happy but at other times you see the guards not looking so jolly. Some people may think, "oh that's an easy job, just walking around saying hello to everyone", but that's not true. The security officer in a medium-sized shopping centre could walk an average of 15-30 km a day on a 12-hour day shift. Guards on night shift, however, do tend to walk way less than that due to minimum activity in the centre outside of opening hours.

The day shift officers work really hard on their feet and some days they get to have very little break time due to the number of incidents they have to attend to. Due to the amount of walking around required, a lot of security guards will not accept jobs in retail environments. Many within a short period of time quit working in retail and go into another area of security that does not require a lot of walking.

Static officers: How about when you're walking into your local store and you see that security officer standing at the door saying 'welcome' with a smile on their face! Well, that's a static security officer. That's another tough job to do standing on your feet for 8-12 hours per shift in a single spot except for a few stores that may allow you to roam around once in a while or if there is a suspicious person in the store.

Static security is one of the security responsibilities that are most hated in the industry. A lot of officers who are into static security tend not to be full-time and tend to be new guards looking to gain experience, who after a few months move to some other form of security.

Static security gets a bit boring because most times the officer works alone. Time goes slowly and you get a sore back and really sore feet, so, for this reason, many guards decline to work in retail security.

Risk: I want to be careful not to scare people away from retail security, but I must stress the fact that, it's a job filled with risk, like any other job.

I know a lot of people who work in nightclubs, cash in transit (CIT), hospitals or certain other types of security may feel their kind of security is riskier, and you may be right. However, I will shed some light on the risks associated with retail security.

Suburb dependant: If you are working in a shopping centre or retail environment that's in a well-to-do or rich suburb, the risk tends to be really low. This is due to the fact that the patrons visiting the shops are most likely well-off and not hustling to live. On the other hand, if the retail environment is in a suburb where a lot of the residents are on welfare or people are struggling to survive, then welcome to Trouble Street.

Suburbs that are not well-off have a higher crime rate than wealthier suburbs. Such crime rates correlate with patrons who are desperate or affected by drugs. Teenagers who come from these tough home environments with no positive role model around them tend to always hang around such shopping centres, shoplifting, assaulting people or just generally causing trouble for other patrons increasing the risk for the security officers.

Lack of respect: I have worked in several types of security and in different roles but the one I know for sure where security officers are the most disrespected is in the retail environment.

These officers may be dealing with patrons with mental challenges, patrons who are outright rude, unruly teenagers, rude retailer or contractor staff who think the security officer is a uniformed drone.

I believe it's possible for me to write a book on the issue of lack of respect for the security officer in the retail environment when compared to other security environments.

Health reasons: Being a retail security officer requires some degree of being in good health, because the officer would not only be walking a lot but will be dealing with a lot of conflict resolution, restraining of aggressive, violent people and sometimes running to attend emergency situations.

So many officers having health challenges tend to avoid retail security and I think they are wise to make such decisions. Health comes before wealth.

FANTASTIC EXPERIENCES!

If as a person you always desire adventure, a job that's not boring, and there is always something to do, or you want a rich work and life experience, then I will recommend you do retail security.

Yes, it's harder than most other security jobs and there are risks involved, but it's also very rewarding and there are great experiences to be had and great friends to be made. Whether it's the delivery drivers, casual leasing staff, cleaning team, customers, management, police or what have you, I can assure you that it's a great job and only a few jobs beat the experience and adventure you will have as retail security officer!

STORY
Thief and a Con Artist

I have had the opportunity to witness a lot of situations/events as a security officer. Things that sometimes make you think it's a movie script being played out right before your eyes, but suddenly you realise, no, this is a real-life situation. And plenty of scenes witnessed are just straight-out hilarious and comedic!

Now this individual is someone who each time I see him at my place of work, I can't help but chuckle because I knew him really well. He has all sorts of tricks up his sleeve for committing an offence or separating others from their items.

I will call him Pablo (not real name). He lives very near to where I work which we found out as a result of one of his thieving sprees when he suddenly ran into his house across the road after fleeing from the scene of the crime.

Pablo is a man roughly in his early fifties or thereabouts. He comes to the centre quite often and he's always calm, smooth-talking, and never violent but just waiting for the right opportunity.

FIRST ENCOUNTER

I remember him one day walking to the receptionist and saying he had lost a wallet. Then he left the reception area and walked around the food court area. He walked past a customer who was sitting on one of the chairs enjoying their meal with their wallet on the same table. Pablo walked past, then sighted the customer's wallet and decided it's best he takes it off the customer. He grabbed the wallet and started running. The customer was so stunned that they could not even chase him. A few teenagers saw what happened and chased Pablo but he took a sharp right corner where a jewellery store was and hid inside acting like he was a customer. The youths had no idea where Pablo went because it was a crossed intersection and they went the wrong way. Pablo came out of the jewellery store this time walking because he had seen the teens run straight past and then he exited the centre.

Security was able to follow all events in real-time via CCTV, and while the teens were fast to respond, security was also following what was going on with cameras. Other guards were dispatched to go after Pablo, as we knew exactly where he was and also where he was heading, even if we were a little behind.

Pablo was followed to the car park and then he went across the road into his home. We could not go across the road because that's outside of our licensed premises, so the police were called and Pablo was arrested right inside his house. I am not sure he knew security saw him entering his house. I am sure if he had known, he would have faked it and entered the wrong house or walked past his house, or perhaps he did know and was just acting plain stupid?

OTHER ENCOUNTERS

Pablo just had this run of consistent thieving. Each time he came in he made efforts to steal, and he didn't just steal a little. He stole stock that would fetch him good money and that would sell really quickly.

On this one occasion when he came into the centre, with his calm personality. He walked into a retail store, grabbed a flat-screen TV, placed it on a trolley and started walking away. He's so natural in how he steals; he doesn't panic or let his body language betray him. That's how good he was. Security was immediately called about the theft because most retailers won't bother to follow an offender after a certain distance. Our camera operator was able to ascertain who it was and their current location, then we went after him and retrieved the TV off of him. He didn't argue with us, he just drops it and continues walking as calm as a chameleon.

Side note: Part of our policy where I work, is not to make an arrest unless it's an extremely exceptional situation, otherwise it's very rare we would physically arrest an offender. As long as we retrieve the retailer's stock then we are happy. If we are unable to then we pass over the incident report to the police to deal with.

MORE ENCOUNTERS WITH PABLO

Another day with Pablo around and I guessed it wouldn't be a boring day at work! On this day, he stole a few electrical gadgets from a major retailer, but before security was informed about the theft, he'd already left the centre. An hour later he returned to the centre and the woman in the retail store recognised him and called security.

This time he could not steal anything as the store closely monitored him. He immediately left and went to the centre library nearby. We checked cameras and were 100% sure Pablo was in the library. We refused to confront him there about his earlier theft in the day so we decided to call the police. The police took a bit of a while to come but when they did, we made sure we provided them with printed photos of Pablo with stolen items in his possession. The police were convinced he had stolen and after I led the police to Pablo at the library he was placed under arrest.

YEARS LATER

I was walking around roving on a sunny winter's day when a retailer called me and said there's this man asking people for money in the centre. A lot of retailers and customers don't feel comfortable when others come begging for money because we have seen so many phoney characters around doing that. Each time we receive such complaints we approach the people carrying out the act and try to let them know of the complaints made by the centre's retailers and patrons.

I decided to approach the male who was accused of begging for money and he kind of looked familiar. I tried to recall where I knew him from, and oh, it's Pablo. This time he seems to have lost a lot of weight and was looking in worse shape than before.

I said, "hey buddy, what's going on?", and he said he'd just got a call from his brother from country Victoria hundreds of kilometres away. Their mum had just had a heart attack and he was begging people for money to catch a train there, with tears in his eyes!

I said I was sorry to hear that but to please stop asking people for money in the centre as it's not allowed here. I also asked if I could call his brother and speak to him. He said no, that his brother works in a prison and he just used the prison phone to ring him but he hasn't got a phone number to reach him on. So, I said I would pay for a taxi to take Pablo there even though it's far and could possibly cost me hundreds of dollars. Pablo responded that is was kind of me but that he would prefer cash. I told him nope, I wouldn't give him any cash and that he had to leave the centre now because we knew him from years ago for shoplifting and that he was now just attempting a different strategy.

Pablo wasn't too happy I busted his plans and we escorted him out of the centre.

A few weeks later, I saw him trying to pull another trick with some dodgy briefcase in the centre and we stopped him and I asked him how's your mum doing and he replied, "oh, she died three years ago". I am sure he forgot what he told me and the other patrons the last time we saw him.

STORY
The Day I Felt Like Quitting

Wouldn't it be great if our workplace was all just nice and cosy? We did our jobs and then returned home all happy and waited for our pay check.

Yes, most times at work we tend to enjoy our days, except maybe if you're in the wrong job or working with the wrong set of people. Most people, I believe, have the majority of their working days going smoothly and beautifully with not many things to complain about.

Nevertheless, what about the days at work where we think everything and everyone is against us? When things are just not going our way even though we are doing all the right stuff. That has been my work situation on so many occasions. Times I feel like just taking a few days off, calling in sick, times I feel like it's best I look for another job altogether, or times when work becomes something else and you contemplate quitting!

I remember this very day, walking on the site scanning my surroundings hoping I could find something suspicious, somebody who may need help or sometimes just walking checking the floor to see if I could find any spill or hazard to isolate so no one gets hurt. That's basically what roving patrol is all about at our site. On this occasion, close to the fruit shop I found some grapes on the floor. I pushed them under the fruit barrel so no one would slip on the grapes because you know grapes and tiles don't mix.

One of the men in the fruit shop came to me and was I expecting him to thank me for my work. Instead, he came and said, "don't ever kick the grapes again". I said to him, "I just did that to help your customers and the shopping centre patrons so they wouldn't slip on them", but he still wouldn't accept that and became really rude.

A FEW HOURS LATER

I was doing my patrol when I came across a retailer asking two teenagers to return to her store, but they wouldn't even bother turning back to listen. The retailer told me they had stolen some clothing items and asked me to follow them and retrieve them for her. I said I was sorry but that I couldn't because I didn't see them steal the items and that she would have to come with me as a witness. As previously mentioned, it's standard procedure not to go on my own after any offender based purely on someone else's claims. I must have witnessed it myself or seen a photo or CCTV evidence. Then I can go after the offender myself but if not, the witness, in this case, the retailer, has to come with me and ask for the item themselves while I back them up.

But this retailer wouldn't even listen to me explaining our security standard procedure and she started calling me names. I called my supervisor so he could explain to the retailer the procedures but still, she wouldn't listen to anyone and even became more vile and rude towards security.

SOMETIME LATER THE SAME DAY

I was called to assist a retailer who was having a dispute with some patrons. According to the retailer, these two male patrons were acting suspiciously. I got to the store and I found the retailer and the patrons arguing. The retailer was accusing them of trying to steal. She searched them and couldn't find anything on them and the men were unhappy with the false accusation.

My job was to try and de-escalate the situation and try to be fair to both the parties. The situation was a bit difficult because of the retailer making false accusations against the patrons. I am employed by the centre, so I have to tread carefully and calm the patrons without making the retailer feel slighted, even though in this case she was wrong with her accusation. I also have to the make the patrons feel they have been heard and treated fairly.

I asked the patrons to come outside the store so we could chat. They agreed and demanded to see the store CCTV footage that shows them stealing or attempting to steal. I informed them I work for the whole centre so I have got no access to the retailer's CCTV. I explained to them if they felt unfairly treated that they can forward their complaint to the retailer's head office via their website.

The two males were happy with my resolution and they left. I went inside the store to let the retailer know what I had discussed with the patrons. Within a split second the retailer twisted my words and said I told the customers the retailer doesn't have in-store CCTV. I was shocked by how quickly she twisted my words, but she stood her ground saying that's what I had told her that I had said to the customers. I tried to explain and again she wouldn't even listen to me.

She made me feel like I was enabling the customers, even though she was the person at fault for falsely accusing the patrons of theft. I'd tried my best to assist her by getting the patrons to leave her store and now I had become the bad guy!

I felt terribly sad the whole day. Here I was trying to assist people/retailers with good intent and all three of them in the one day had rejected my assistance, called me names and falsely accused me.

The whole week I was just thinking of how people misinterpret my intentions and how some people act in a disrespectful way towards security officers! However, I did eventually bounce back not long after because I wouldn't allow the way I was badly treated hold me down!

I have had plenty of days like this on so many occasions, but such days make you stronger by the life experience you gain from these unpleasant situations.

Chapter Sixteen

SECURITY OFFICER'S PAY AND ENTITLEMENTS

I have spoken to a lot of people in the industry. One of the most common concerns is that most people come into the industry as a 'Plan B', meaning they are planning on doing security just for the time being until they get into their dream career. Or they got laid off from their previous job, lost their business or are a new immigrant. Whatever the circumstances, a good number of these people end up staying in the industry, either through choice, their age or some other personal reason.

GOOD PAY

The security industry award wage in Australia is uniform, but there are different areas of security and their pay scale varies. For example, armed guards, aviation security, port security, bodyguards and crowd control, just to mention a few. Security also has different ratings or levels. Often such levels are measured by the amount of hazard you're most likely to face or the responsibilities and work you will carry out and that determines the pay, although none of them are below the security award wage.

Take, for example, a guard I used to work with in port security who earns about $120,000 per annum before tax, whereas in another retail site the supervisor/manager earns about $62,000 annually before tax.

So, as you can see, it depends on what area/level of security you work in. Sometimes it depends on the company or the contract that the employer has. For example, security officers for the Reserve Bank tend to be paid really high wages, but this job is not an easy one to get into as it requires a lot of high-security clearance and you must have the right certification. Sometimes it's who you know that can help you to secure a good, high paying job.

So, in the industry, there are a lot of high paying jobs above $60,000 a year as a basic security officer. Sometimes it depends on the number of hours you are able to work, your training/certification, experience, employer and the site you work in.

PAYING LESS

Another group of people I have come across are the ones sitting on the fence. Either they are planning to join the industry or they already have their licence and they're busy shopping around asking questions like, 'how much are you being paid?'. They are not wrong to ask such questions so as to be sure what they are getting into. You can't blame them when the Australian security industry award wage promises more, but a lot of shonky operators try to get away with paying less, otherwise known as wage theft.

DODGY AND DESPERATE OPERATORS

Lack of a united voice and desperation is what is robbing the trained and licensed security officer their rightful wage. If all security officers are paid the right wage as set by the Fair Work Commission under the Security Services Award in Australia, the security officer would have to be one of the best-paid occupations in the country.

Sadly, the industry is filled with a lot of greedy individuals (aka operators, companies, businesses) who only think of their pockets and not the employee. Such desperation to secure jobs/contracts from clients has made a lot of these operators in a bidding war to the lowest possible denominator in what rate they charge the client. Often, it's even below the award wage just in order to get jobs/contracts, undercutting legitimate and reputable companies who charge clients a certain rate so they can pay their employees the legal wage and cover their own costs. At the end of the day, 'the little man', the security officer pays the ultimate cost by being underpaid, below the national minimum wage. Take note, minimum wage is not the same as the Security Services Industry Award wage.

These low bids from questionable operators mean that they can't afford to pay their security officer the award wage. Their aim for such low bids to the client is to win jobs/contracts and make profits but then the client is supplied guards who are not properly trained, not suitable for the jobs and roles available. Also these guards are not motivated because they know they are being ripped off. Their output becomes abysmal and the client loses customers due to security personnel underperforming or in some cases, these operators even supply untrained and unlicensed individuals as security personnel.

If operators in the security industry can be united in their resolve to clean up the industry and pay all security officers award wage, only putting in bids for jobs/contracts that will afford them to pay the right award wage, the security industry will attract higher IQ (intelligence quotient) and EQ (emotional intelligence) individuals to join the industry and also retain the great guards already in the industry.

WHAT TO DO?

<u>Research</u>: There are a few security companies that pay award wage, but many don't. I would encourage you, the security officer, to undertake a bit of research about such companies and seek to work for them.

<u>Stand in unity</u>: When you work for a questionable operator, I urge you to talk to your colleagues about the unfair wage you're being paid. Band yourselves together, join a union and approach the employer to review your wage in line with the national security industry award.

Report to authorities: Report the employers to the Fair Work Commission or any national statutory body that regulates or oversees the wages of workers.

Don't work for them: If you're already working for a questionable business, make an exit plan of how to find an employer that pays the right wage, or if you're looking for a job, do your research and don't take jobs with companies that are underpaying their guards.

IT'S HARD

I know having just said all this, that it's hard to find or keep a job, and as the proverb goes, 'beggars can't be choosers'. I would encourage you to seek opportunities to start your own business or consider changing careers. But, before you take any step, make sure you do your homework well. Consult others for right counsel and be sure you're 100% certain you are taking the right steps for change.

WHY SECURITY PERSONNEL MUST BE PAID RIGHT - LINE OF DEFENCE FOR THE CLIENT

The security of every organisation, business or a nation starts with the individual. If the individual employee, resident or patron decided to do what is right and what is expected of them in the first instance, then there would be fewer security concerns.

If employees, residents and patrons decided to be more vigilant, active and personally responsible for the security of their place of employment or residence then we would have fewer worries about security issues. Security starts with you. Whether you're in security or not, it starts with you doing the right thing and taking more personal responsibility for the security of your current environment.

THE OFFICER'S DEFENCE

One of the most important assets you will have in your business is your investment in your business security infrastructure. Be it securing your organisation's information and communications technology (ICT) equipment or getting the correctly paid security personnel to patrol the gate of your offices/business.

THE CLIENT HAS TO PAY

When I talk about how you as the individual are the number one security person, when you take a responsible approach to looking after your organisation or place of residence, this also means every security officer that is employed at your organisation is as important as every single employee you have on your books.

You may assume security officers are just little people who mean nothing more than someone to provide customer service and open gates, etc., but they mean far more than that.

The security officers who are looking after your investment have a great deal more responsibility placed on them than a lot of managers at your workplace. When you go home at night your organisation is totally in the hands of these trained and paid officers who will not sleep but keep an eye on your business and make sure it is secured. If there is any attempt of intrusion or suspicious behaviour, they will call the local police for assistance.

DATA

The security officer has access to a lot of an organisation's data, and access that only a few top executive and managers are given. They work night and day to secure this data and make sure that no unauthorised person has access to such valuable information.

HAZARD

Security officers do not only work to protect and secure your property, but they also act as ad-hoc health and safety officers, reporting and removing potential hazards as to avoid an employee or patrons getting hurt. This saves the company a lot of money in accident payouts and legal fees.

VALUE AND MOTIVATION

Most businesses these days hire security companies to supply them with security personnel or hardware. One thing you have to consider is when you contract these officers, they are now part of your organisation for the duration of the job/contract. As such, you should make these officers feel they are a part of your organisation. That makes them feel more valued and gives them that extra motivation to give a 100% in all they do. Even going above and beyond in the service they provide to your business.

<u>Value</u>: Here in Australia, there is the national Security Services Industry Award (feel free to Google the current one) which will give you an idea of how much each individual officer ought to be paid. Also try to ascertain what security level the guards employed will be performing at in your organisation. The more tasks or the more complex the tasks/responsibilities the officers will be required to perform, the higher the rating of their duties goes up. For example; control room duties, fire installation panel checks, screening of visitors/patrons, etc. The more the level increases, the more the security guard should be paid. If you are not sure what level you or your business security needs are, do some research on the internet or contact the Australian Security Industry Association (ASIAL).

Do your research properly to find how much the award wage is and what the security level is. Get the right security contractors and ask them how much they will be paying the officers employed for your business. If possible, set the rate of how much they will be paid and ask your potential contractors to add their running and other costs to the total bill.

DON'T TAKE THE RISK

I know every business is always looking to cut costs and maximise profit. When it comes to the security of your property, business and country, do not toy with wanting to cut costs that will compromise safety standards. Get the best security company regardless of how much they may charge. There are lots of companies who will offer you the same services for a very low, ridiculous price where the guards who will be securing your property, business or national infrastructure are seriously underpaid. They are illegally underpaying staff, which sooner or later will force officers to take the security contractor to the ombudsman. That will end up costing the contractor more money in back pay and negative publicity for both the security company and on your business.

Don't go for the low bidding contractor. Go for a contractor that pays your guards the right, legal wage and always follow up with the security officers on a regular basis to check they are being paid the legal rate.

Motivation: When the officers at your organisation know they are paid what they are entitled to, they feel respected and valued. n return, they feel much more motivated to give you all they've got and take responsibility in being the eyes and ears of your business to keep it safe and secured.

Danger of less motivated officers: It is better not to have security officers at your business at all than to have guards who are consistently unhappy at work. They are constantly sweating and toiling while knowing they are being ripped off and not paid the right wage.

The saying goes in the industry, 'you only get the service you pay for'. When you pay the guard 70% of what they're meant to earn, they will give you 70% of the service that you deserve. This is a fact!

Weak link: When your competitor wants to come after you, they will come through the weak link in your organisation. In the same way, when criminals or terrorists want to come after any business or national infrastructure (airports, seaports, etc.), they come after the weak link. Your security personnel, who are unmotivated because they are underpaid and they do not feel valued, they are like a goldmine for your competitors. Criminals or terrorists could infiltrate your business to get data or gain access to materials which could cause you losses or harm. If you fail to pay the security guards right, they could get paid by these unwanted criminals and cause your business harm.

Disclaimer: This is not to imply that security personnel are conduits for criminal activities, no that's not true. A great majority of security officers are honest, love their jobs and will do anything to protect any business that has been entrusted into their hands to look after. Rather the purpose is to shed more light on the dangers of underpaying or hiring a sham security contractor.

STORY
The Undesirable Haircut

If my workplaces hadn't offered me so many great opportunities to laugh, wonder and ponder, along with a few challenging moments, I am sure I would have found being a security officer a boring profession.

While working, I have witnessed people do a lot of unbelievable things. I have seen a man snatch a bag from a female who was so shocked by the brazen act of desperation, she could not move from her seat to chase the offender! I have seen a female snatch a $50 note from the hands of a patron and started running as if she just won a lottery. Not to downplay the customer who went and ordered the best and tastiest food from a restaurant, then did a runner when it was time to pay!

I have seen quite a lot, that sometimes surprised me and other times I just wondered what might have gone wrong in the mind and life of someone to make the offending individual want to pull such acts.

BACK TO THE STORY

This was sad and funny! This young man decided to go into one of the premium boutique barbershops. This particular barbershop knows how to turn any hair and head into looking really good. I mean they have mastered the art of the haircut and they also come with a hefty rate for anyone wanting to get their hair done.

The young man went in for a haircut and the barber took his time to skilfully worked on the hair of the customer. The barber made sure he made his customer look really good and gave him the exact hairstyle and cut he desired. He made him look really handsome and stylish. I mean a haircut that anyone who sees it would know for sure, a master craftsman did work on this hair!

After each customers hair has been cut, you are then directed to go to the front desk and make payment. However, this particular male had another idea; he loved the hairstyle but didn't want to pay for it!

The male decided to do a runner within the shopping centre and the barber who worked on his hair also equally decided he wouldn't let him get away. He ran after him with one of the cordless-clippers, he caught up with the running male, held him really tight and firm. The barber decided to re-shape his hair cut into one that was undesirable! A hairstyle that he would be ashamed to let anyone see and would have to get another barber to shave every hair he has on his head.

Well, the barber shop did not get their money, but they made sure he didn't leave looking cute!

Chapter Seventeen

HOW TO LOSE YOUR SECURITY JOB

This chapter will discuss some, not all, of the actions, attitudes and character traits that if a security officer possesses, displays or develops will make it hard for them to keep their job.

The purpose is not to encourage the security officer to lose what they have but to point out that having such negative character traits or behaviour will definitely put any officer into having to search the available job market.

Some of the points I will discuss are things I have witnessed in the industry; officers who were demoted, others who lost their jobs entirely. Including some who had to travel far distances from home to work because their negative attitude had been found out by the closest potential employer to them!

Being professional at all times and having a good work attitude saves you a lot of 'please explain, see me in the office' kind of emails from bosses or management.

I hope by the time you read this, you will be more eager to check yourself and see the areas you think you can improve on. Have a better idea of the attitudes and behaviour you feel you need to drop so you can keep your job, and not only to just keep your job, but excel in your career as a security guard.

<u>Drugs and drinking</u>: Doing drugs in most countries and territories is a crime. Doing them at work or coming to work affected by drugs would most likely get you fired. And how about drinking? Take note, I am not saying all drinking is bad, I am talking about people who have a problem with alcohol. Those who sometimes come to work with a hangover or are still kind of drunk and also the few who actually hide somewhere to consume alcohol while at work.

I use myself as an example. I am most effective in all I do since I quit drinking alcohol altogether. I work more, call less sick days or take time off work and I tend to have a sharper mind while on the job. Equally, my weekends now are always very productive too and I'm a good husband to my wife and father to my kids.

Now not everyone has to be like me and there are those who have great self-control and are good at drinking an amount that's right for them. Kudos to such people! But what about those who have real issues with alcohol, where liquor affects them negatively in almost every area of their lives? What about those who can hardly stop once they start drinking and whose work and workmates suffer for it because they end up not showing up for work or when they do they are only half as good?

Likewise, the danger is, if you do drugs I doubt you will be able to do your job properly or keep your employment. When I talk about drugs, I am talking about illegal or recreational substances, such as methamphetamine (ice), heroin, cocaine and other dangerous drugs that numb the mind or turn sane people into some kind of zombies.

So, don't do drugs, and not just because of the effect on your work life. Think of yourself, and of your family and loved ones who would want to relate with a better you. As for alcohol, it's not for everyone, and even if you think it's for you, don't abuse it. Know the times and seasons to drink. Drink for a good reason and not because you think it will help you to solve your problems. I have never heard of or seen anyone who has solved their life issues and problems by drinking alcohol or taking drugs.

If you are going through life difficulties or challenges, take note others are facing similar or even worse. The difference is, they may be seeking help from family, friends and most importantly qualified professionals who can help them to overcome such challenges of life.

There are professional counsellors, psychologists and life coaches who can be of help to you and sometimes trusted friends can be of help. But don't just shut yourself away and think the pills or bottle can help solve your problems.

<u>Sleeping on shift</u>: This is one big issue in the industry, where guards show up for a night shift, sometimes an 8-hour shift but most times 12 hours long, and all they do throughout the shift is either watch Netflix or YouTube and then sleep.

You have to understand you are paid to keep an eye on the property, business or premises you are there to look after and are not being paid to come and have some sleep.

<u>True story</u>: I know of a guard who almost every time he works night shift, he goes to his station and every two hours that he's expected to patrol his area and then call on the radio, this particular guard sleeps and every two hours wakes up and calls 'patrol complete', but he never does the patrol.

He kept on doing that for a long time, even though there is a security camera where he's stationed. The time came when the security business had to cut costs. To do so they had to get rid of a security guard and guess who was first on the chopping block? You guessed right, the sleeping guard. He was asked to resign as an honourable way to dismiss him. The company only had to use several days of CCTV footage and show the guard he wasn't doing patrols even though he always called 'patrol complete'.

If you have issues keeping awake at night, then it's best not to accept jobs or shifts that require you to work overnight, because it is unethical to accept and then come to work and start sleeping on the job.

<u>Failing to do patrols</u>: This issue is also a big problem in the industry, where guards are employed as patrol officers, given a patrol vehicle and equipment to do patrols but the guard never completes their patrols, or sometimes uses company patrols vehicles to go on their own personal pursuits or errands.

Although a lot of companies have implemented many tracking, wand or advanced technologies to keep track of their officer's runs, you always get this clever-lazy officer who has a device that enables them to beat those checks.

Though the officer may think they are smart, they will be caught out when an incident happens at a particular place they were expected to patrol and they fail to report it to the control room or site and then they lose their employment.

My advice is, keep your job and stay awake, because your employer can only keep the contract with you when you stay awake and do the job you are hired or employed to do.

<u>Late coming</u>: Arriving early or in time for work or any occasion, says a lot about you. It shows a side of you that is: dedicated, consistent, serious, mature and trustworthy, all by that simple act of showing up to work early or on any occasion.

You are most likely a super-nice and sweet person, but when you are known for late coming, it doesn't paint you in a good light. It shows a not so subtle character trait that you don't take things really seriously and as a consequence, people may not trust you when it comes to something important.

You may come late and leave late thinking you are covering for your lateness by staying behind, but first impressions matter and that first impression is, 'what time did you arrive at work?'

So, if any employer or workmate wants to find anything against you later on, they could use your lateness against you, and some employers won't tolerate such negative work traits.

Picking up: This sad situation is prevalent among a small minority of security guards in the industry. They think or assume their uniform and 'position of authority' gives them the right to turn their workplace and position into some kind of 'Tinder' set up. A lot of security officers have lost their jobs because they lost focus and got distracted from their original purpose of employment (to observe and report) and instead they invest so much effort in wanting to find a hook-up while at work.

A lot of security officers who display this appalling behaviour in most sites or workplaces tend to be ill-disciplined, and lack self-control and direction because all their energy and focus is dedicated to wanting to pick-up someone and take them home for the night or day. Sometimes they keep it within the bounds of fellow guards but on most occasions, such negative behaviour is directed towards the customers or clients.

I am not trying to say a guard cannot meet their future partner at work; no that's not what I am talking about. What I am talking about are the desperate and loose officers whose intention and focus is to find or pick-up someone for a hook-up.

Yes, many security officers have lost their jobs and even their licence because they forgot why they are employed and focused more on wanting to find a hook-up.

Rudeness: As mentioned in a previous chapter, the security job in this day and age entails a high level of customer service. The officer's ability to deliver exceptional customer assistance to each and every individual that patronises the business or premises of the client.

Customer service also means being polite in almost every situation towards the client and patron. Therefore, as a security officer, you must realise that being rude or responding to customers or clients in a rude manner would most definitely get you suspended or kicked out of your place of employment.

From firsthand experience, I have seen a lot of people in the security industry who got kicked out of a site or entirely lost their job because of their inability to be cool under pressure or were consistently being rude to clients and customers.

So, my advice is, rudeness and customer service are like water and oil, they never mix or go hand in hand. Don't take things personally, and always remember it's a job you are doing and you are representing a brand and a business and not yourself.

STORY
Security Officer Coming to Steal

When a crime-preventer takes off their uniform and decides to become someone who commits the crime, then you get to ask yourself, 'what went wrong?'

I was at work when I got this phone call from a retailer; they had just had a theft, so I went in there and had a chat with the retailer who looked not so happy. Her stock had been stolen and she was looking to me to do something about it.

I told her I would check the CCTV and I took her details and description of the offenders. I went to the office and checked the cameras and realised the offenders were a male and female who had left the centre. I was disappointed that they had already left, so all that was left was for me to do the incident report and for the retailer to call to police and make a report.

WEEKS LATER

I was patrolling again in the centre when I got a call from an unknown number. I was busy attending to other patrons so I could not pick the call.

Minutes had gone by and I was informed the woman from the store wants to see me. I went into the store and the retailer told me a couple came into her store and stole some items. I swung into action straight away, checked the cameras, and well it's my 'old friends' from a few weeks before. This time after they stole, they went into another store, so they were still in the centre.

I went into the store and I said to the male, "hey buddy, can you come with me to the store you just left?" He acted like he didn't hear what I said so I went closer, then he said, "please don't embarrass me, and my wife is having severe depression". Well, I just stood there calmly and waited for them to come with me.

They had stolen two expensive women's handbags but he gave me only one back and he said that's what they had on them. Then I reminded him of their theft a few weeks ago and he started panicking and his wife started acting strangely. He pleaded with me for his wife not to return to the store as she was having 'severe depression'. I agreed and I told him I am going to call the police for the previous theft and he said, "Look, I am an off-duty loss prevention officer. I'm willing to pay for the previous theft and return all I stole today". I was happy with his proposal and allowed him to pay for what they stole a few weeks earlier. The retailer was happy with the result and I evicted them out of the centre.

Surprise. A man who earns his money preventing theft and apprehending thieves ends up being a thief himself. Who knows what he does at his place of employment; that's a story for another day.

STORY
Employee Losing Job for Stealing

Being a security officer also means being professional at all times. There are days when you are faced with certain situations where being professional then becomes cumbersome. Even so, you have no choice but to be professional at all times and do what you are employed and expected to do. A few people may hate you for being professional and sticking to the books, but most people will trust you for being professional.

I was almost done with work for the day, and then we got a call that a customer had lost their shopping trolley in the toilets.

I decided to review the cameras, hoping to see another customer walking away with the items as it's usually the case in such situations, but I was surprised to find a cleaner took the items and kind of hid them in their cleaning trolley. You see when someone is plotting a sinister act; most times from their body language you can tell.

I followed the cleaner on the camera and discovered the items kept getting transferred from one cover to the other. It was never reported to the cleaner's manager as lost property, and I had to put in a report about it based on what I had witnessed.

The cleaner was called the next day about the items, some of which they had already taken home, but the cleaner claimed they didn't steal the items. The cleaner was given the opportunity to acknowledge what they did, but they kept denying it, even with obvious camera evidence. Then the cleaner decided to resign, instead of acknowledging what they did. In total, the items were worth not more than $60, but sadly they ended up losing their job that was worth thousands of dollars a year.

Chapter Eighteen

BE AHEAD, STUDY MORE

A lot of security officers sit in the office and wonder what's going on; how can I get ahead and stay ahead in this industry? I have been doing this job for years and there seems to be no career progression, limited opportunities and I'm doing the same thing over and over. That's one of the hard questions many security officers often ask: why can't I have career progression in this industry?

Humans have always been ambitious, wanting advancement in their life or work. Sometimes an employee's productivity tends to drop off because the officer feels discouraged. They aren't being promoted, or they've applied for so many jobs that could take their career in the industry to the next level, but they always get rejected in spite of their industry experience.

HOW DO WE FIX THIS?

Experience is good and it's a great thing to have, but don't forget sometimes experience has got its limitations too without the right qualifications and training. I always advise security officers to not just have the basic entry qualification of the industry and think years of experience will take you to your dream position or opportunity.

Experience is good but sometimes you will get hamstrung when faced with the superior qualifications of a less experienced officer in a job interview.

Increasing qualifications: Try and improve on your current qualification, and if possible, get something that is around twice as high as your current qualification. For example, if you have a Certificate III, go for a Certificate IV or a Diploma. If you currently possess a Diploma, go for an Advanced Diploma or a Bachelor's Degree. Don't just sit and complain. If you have the desire and the dream to advance yourself in the industry, try and advance your current qualification and don't just rely solely on your experience.

YOU CAN DO IT

Sometimes people who are supervising or managing you are less talented and skilled than you are, but because they may have more qualifications than you or maybe due to who they know or that they have been there before you, you find yourself in that situation.

Let that be a motivating factor for you to recommence study again. Don't say, 'I am unintelligent, old or not smart enough to study'. Go to most colleges, universities and training institutes and you would find people in a worse situation than you studying and graduating through sheer determination and hard work.

Secondary qualifications: There are a lot of secondary certifications and qualifications that would help enhance your current security qualification (e.g. Control Room Certificate, Health and Safety Certificate, Certificate in Training and Assessment, Advanced First Aid, Advanced Fire Warden Certificate, etc.). Sometimes that might be what you need to add to your security qualification that could give you that extra boost to further your career in the industry.

Conduct your own research and see what extra secondary qualification/certification could be of help to further move your career forward either in the security industry or elsewhere.

Study online: Perhaps you may say, I have got a family that needs to be fed and I can't afford to go back to university or college, etc. Well, if you can't go to the mountain, the mountain can come to you.

There are many universities, colleges and training institutes that offer government approved courses that you could do online. By spending just 4-8 hours a week studying, within 8 months you could obtain a diploma, or in a couple of years, you could have a Bachelor's Degree while you are still working.

But remember, while online study gives you the flexibility to study at your own pace, a lot of self-discipline is also required to complete your course.

Networking: People say, 'in most jobs, it's who you know'. They can't be far from the truth, however, I believe you may know someone but without the right qualification you won't get the job, and I believe it is best you occupy a position you know you are duly qualified for it and not just because of who you know.

It is important to network, whether via industry groups on Facebook, LinkedIn or other community groups. No person is an island, and in our lifetime, we will at least need someone we know to give us a push in time of need, especially when it comes to employment or career progression.

NUGGET & STORY
Playing on the Psyche of the Offender

BEFORE THE STORY

The intending offending patron at your site or premises is always thinking ahead and always inventing new ways to carry out their crime.

Often the security officer is left to be more or less a student of the offender, always learning after the offence has already been carried out.

But that should not always be the case, because as a security officer you are not just only employed to 'observe and report', but also to bring new techniques and concepts of doing security that are in line with the governing statutes and regulations that guide the security industry.

If we as officers of the industry are just there to 'observe and report', I believe then our role is archaic and somewhat naive. If the criminal is always thinking ahead, then I believe the security officer should be thinking three times more ahead. Always imagining scenarios and ways breaches and offences could occur at their place of employment and how they could stop that from happening. In other words, you are there to mitigate risk.

The security officer in the 21st century must not just walk around and be seen, but also try to be creative and be a thinker. Think about how to confront unknown situations, not only known situations. When confronted with a difficult situation, you must be able to think swiftly outside the box and pull out creative ideas that could be the solution to the difficulty you are being confronted with.

No matter what type of security you do, the uniform and job title of 'security', should not limit who you are as a person. Who you are is more important than the uniform and name 'security' that's been placed on you due to your current circumstantial need to earn a living by being a security officer.

You have a brilliant and intelligent mind, wearing a security uniform trying to earn wages. You may be doing security for a season, but for that season you are employed as a security officer you are to give security your best shot, displaying brilliance, intelligence, self-awareness, hard work and empathy.

Security is an occupation, so take it seriously but don't let it limit you by thinking you are doing a job society looks down on. When you realise you are gifted and your unique personality is beyond your job description, then what others think of you or your job is absolutely meaningless. You create security, security doesn't define you!

OFFENDERS THOUGHTS

The offender may be able to bamboozle people in order to steal or rob and think perhaps they are ingenious, but I disagree with such thoughts. It is only a shallow minded person with a clouded view of life that thinks stealing or committing an offence is the best way to make a living or supplement their lifestyle.

For you, my friend the security officer, I believe you are more superior in thought, intellect and wisdom than a thief. That's why you chose the 'hard way' to earn a living. It may take you time to achieve your life dreams and goals, but you are surely on the right way to succeeding. When you do succeed in life, it lasts you a lifetime of joy and fulfilment.

THE OFFENDER AND THE OFFICER

Security officers are confronted daily by offenders, who think they are smart, but I find them not to be smart. It is a good thing being a security officer, restrained and guided by legislation and status, as that makes us different from the criminal who operates with no rules.

I will advise you once again to always think quickly and to think brilliantly when you are engaging with an offender to make sure your reaction is in line with the law and with a site's standard operating procedures.

BACK TO MY STORY

I remember this offender (let's call him Jake) who I'd had a previous encounter with before. Jake had walked into a store, picked up a few items of clothing and walked away without paying. He had been doing that consecutively for two days in a row. On the second day, I was fortunate to have been able to catch up with him and I'd asked for the retailer's items back. He refused to return the items and was mocking me and the retailer, but I could not do much because I have to operate within the law and site's policies and procedures.

BACK AGAIN

A few weeks later I got called about a theft; it's Jake again. He walked into a different store this time, stole a number of clothing items and walked away. I caught up with Jake and this time he had a friend/accomplice with him. Jake started laughing at me again, with the stock in his hands, and I thought for a second how do I get these items back before he leaves the centre. I can't use force to retrieve the items, it's against the site's policy.

Jake was approaching the centre exit and I knew the moment he gets to the exit, the items are gone. I decided while behind him, I would pretend to be making a phone call to the police. I made sure I was loud enough on the phone so Jake could hear my conversation and said, "yes, the offender and I are just approaching the exit, wait for us at the centre exit". Immediately, Jake's laughter turned to panic. I then said to Jake, "if you don't want the police to arrest you outside the exit with the stolen items, give them all to me and I will return them to the retailer while you take another exit so you don't get arrested". Well, he thought I was helping him to escape the police! Very panicked, he handed everything over to me and exited a different way.

LESSON LEARNED

On so many occasions, I have used various brain tingling techniques to confront offenders instead of applying illegal force. More often than not, I get positive results and our clients get their stock returned and that saves them money.

Were there police outside? No. The police have always helped us no doubt, but often before the police arrive, the offender has already left the property and the retailer loses their stock.

So, you the security officer, like I said earlier, are intelligent and smart and you must always use your brain power advantage over the offender, and you do have a lot of this.

STORY
Theft, Locked Car, Sheriff

It's been said, 'the owner of a shoe, knows exactly where it hurts'. Allowing naysayers to define who you are is crazy, and accepting their definition is dangerous and foolery. Who you are is best defined by you, and understanding who you are will help to explain your purpose. When you understand your purpose, then you find the freedom to dream dreams and act to turn your dreams to reality!

Your life and its journey; it's like a shoe, and you are the wearer of this shoe (life). So now you have to create your own positive definition of who you are. You alone do that and no one else defines you for you.

STORY BEGINS

Back to the story; it was a normal day at work until I got this call, about some young women who came into the centre and were on a shoplifting spree.

As normal as it is to find locals on their way to do their grocery shopping, so it is for some who purposely go to the shopping centre for a shoplifting spree. I have indeed seen many as such, but I will focus on this particular story I'm about to share, perhaps because the end was peculiar.

The security team and I had been on the trail of these women for a while. We lost track of them but suddenly we got a call; they had struck again and this time I was able to keep a close eye on them.

I started walking behind them, making sure I was close but covert because the report we received was that they had stolen a lot of items. At this moment, I couldn't see them carrying the said 'a lot of items'. It seems they had a vehicle in the car park somewhere where they kept their loot stored before they come back to strike. That was my suspicion because many shoplifters do as much.

Now my aim was to get their car registration and if possible recover all stolen items. I knew it was going be a difficult job to pull off.

My cover had been blown and the women suspected I was following them. They went into the car park and I continued to follow them, but I was unwilling to get too close in case I gave it away that my plan was to get their car registration.

We were all kind of moving in a circle and they seemed to be winning. For my part, I just didn't want to lose track of them and as life would have it, I saw a sheriff patrol car in the car park. The sheriff had just clamped the tire of a vehicle whose owners had failed to pay some government fines. Guess whose car was it? My good 'shoplifting friends' that I'm after!

This change in the situation was a boon! I was able to get the full names of the young women from the sheriff and I also got their car registration. They couldn't drive off because their car had just been clamped.

If not for the sheriff who was in the car park doing their rounds and clamping the particular car of these women, I'm sure I would have gotten tired of going in circles after them and returned back to my duties. Eventually, they would have returned to their car and left.

We also got all the stolen items back and had the police arrest the offenders. What a sweet victory! I was so excited and I believe I would have sung a song of triumph if I was at home!

Chapter Nineteen

LIFE OUTSIDE SECURITY

I met Mr Deon and we had a bit of a chat regarding a business he's trying to introduce to me. I was at work and he'd remarked, "I use to be a security officer many years ago". These days, it's so common to meet a lot of successful people from different industries saying, 'I use to be a security officer'.

It is common, and at the same time, it is an encouragement to the security officer who is thinking of life outside security. It gives hope that there is a positive life outside the industry, that you can succeed in other areas of life if you stop working in security.

I have seen and heard of a lot of security officers who have been able to transition from being a security officer into other fields.

Seb was just a normal guard onsite who did well in his job and as an opportunity came for a new site supervisor he went for it. A few years later he became duty manager working with centre management. How did Seb move that far from being a regular security officer to become a duty manager? You see because Seb has a great amount of knowledge and site experience, he applied for the job and he got it. The last time I am aware of, Seb became the operations manager of a shopping centre worth more than $500 million dollars.

The above story is a true story and there are so many more stories like that I can share with you, to show you there are other opportunities where your security experience can lead you to gain employment there.

POSITIVE FEEDBACK

When you rewrite your resume and go looking for other jobs outside security, in a job that your industry experience could relate to, often that's when you appreciate the importance of your security background. What it also shows to the employer is that you are someone who can be trusted. You are someone who might have worked in tough situations, dealt with difficult people, who has also got practical first aid experience and possesses a great customer service background.

A lot of career options that you could switch to where it would be advantageous for you coming from the security industry are, but not limited to: police, army, fire brigade, paramedics, train driver, customer service personnel, intelligence/spy, community safety officer, building/safety inspector, fire installation technician, parking officer, park ranger, etc.

HOW ABOUT POLITICS

I know a lot of people tend to think all politicians are dishonest, but that's not always true. There are many fine and honest politicians in all political affiliations and parties.

Contesting for local, state or federal elections should not be something too big for you to aim for. You are trying to represent a group of people and as a security officer who has served with distinction, you could tout that as your area of focus for seeking political nomination. As someone able to secure your community and who has a great track record of dealing with offenders/criminals, etc.

I believe a security officer has a very good background to seek the highest office politically. Take, for example, the current president of the Republic of Gambia, Adamah Borrow (as of 2018). He was formerly a Tesco security officer in London before he contested against a sitting president who was a known brutal dictator. His chances of defeating the sitting president were very slim, but he defeated the sitting president and today he is the President of Gambia.

There is no mountain too steep for you to climb as a security officer, be it: starting a business, studying for a PhD, going into politics, changing careers or becoming a law enforcement agent. Being a security officer is only part of your story, so never limit yourself or allow others to, because of your job label 'security officer'. Dream big and aim for the skies so tomorrow others can read your story in history!

www.ingramcontent.com/pod-product-compliance
Lightning Source LLC
Chambersburg PA
CBHW020654300426
44112CB00007B/374